YORK NOTES

Great Expectations

Charles Dickens

Notes by David Langston and
Martin Walker

 Longman   York Press

YORK PRESS
322 Old Brompton Road, London SW5 9JH

ADDISON WESLEY LONGMAN LIMITED
Edinburgh Gate, Harlow,
Essex CM20 2JE, United Kingdom
Associated companies, branches and representatives throughout the world

First published 1997

ISBN 0–582–31339–2

Designed by Vicki Pacey, Trojan Horse
Illustrated by Chris Brown
Map by Neil Cower
Typeset by Pantek Arts, Maidstone, Kent
Phototypeset by Gem Graphics, Trenance, Mawgan Porth, Cornwall
Produced by Longman Asia Limited, Hong Kong
Colour reproduction and film output by Spectrum Colour

CONTENTS

PREFACE

York Notes are designed to give you a broader perspective on works of literature studied at GCSE and equivalent levels. We have carried out extensive research into the needs of the modern literature student prior to publishing this new edition. Our research showed that no existing series fully met students' requirements. Rather than present a single authoritative approach, we have provided alternative viewpoints, empowering students to reach their own interpretations of the text. York Notes provide a close examination of the work and include biographical and historical background, summaries, glossaries, analyses of characters, themes, structure and language, cultural connections and literary terms.

If you look at the Contents page you will see the structure for the series. However, there's no need to read from the beginning to the end as you would with a novel, play, poem or short story. Use the Notes in the way that suits you. Our aim is to help you with your understanding of the work, not to dictate how you should learn.

York Notes are written by English teachers and examiners, with an expert knowledge of the subject. They show you how to succeed in coursework and examination assignments, guiding you through the text and offering practical advice. Questions and comments will extend, test and reinforce your knowledge. Attractive colour design and illustrations improve clarity and understanding, making these Notes easy to use and handy for quick reference.

York Notes are ideal for:
- Essay writing
- Exam preparation
- Class discussion

The authors of these Notes are David Langston and Martin Walker. David Langston (MA) is an English teacher and examiner at GCSE and A level. He has written and contributed to GCSE textbooks. Martin Walker is an English teacher, journalist and NEAB examiner. He has worked on the GCSE examinations in English and English Literature since 1988 and is now a senior examiner.

The edition used in these Notes is the Penguin Classics Edition, 1985, edited by Angus Calder.

Health Warning: This study guide will enhance your understanding, but should not replace the reading of the original text and/or study in class.

INTRODUCTION

HOW TO STUDY A NOVEL

You have bought this book because you wanted to study a novel on your own. This may supplement classwork.

- You will need to read the novel several times. Start by reading it quickly for pleasure, then read it slowly and carefully. Further readings will generate new ideas and help you to memorise the details of the story.
- Make careful notes on themes, plot and characters of the novel. The plot will change some of the characters. Who changes?
- The novel may not present events chronologically. Does the novel you are reading begin at the beginning of the story or does it contain flashbacks and a muddled time sequence? Can you think why?
- How is the story told? Is it narrated by one of the characters or by an all-seeing ('omniscient') narrator?
- Does the same person tell the story all the way through? Or do we see the events through the minds and feelings of a number of different people.
- Which characters does the narrator like? Which characters do you like or dislike? Do your sympathies change during the course of the book? Why? When?
- Any piece of writing (including your notes and essays) is the result of thousands of choices. No book had to be written in just one way: the author could have chosen other words, other phrases, other characters, other events. How could the author of your novel have written the story differently? If events were recounted by a minor character how would this change the novel?

Studying on your own requires self-discipline and a carefully thought-out work plan in order to be effective. Good luck.

The young Dickens experienced the darker side of London life.

Charles Dickens was born in 1812 in Portsmouth. He was the eldest son and one of eight children, two of whom died in childhood. His father, John Dickens, was a clerk in the Navy Pay Office. He did not manage his money well, got into debt and was sent to Marshalsea Prison. He was soon joined there by his wife and five other children. Charles was taken out of school in London and put to work in a filthy warehouse where he had to stick labels on bottles of boot-black. The family had been forced to sell all of their possessions and Charles felt shamed by this. He returned to school for a short time, but this experience left its mark on Dickens. Even years later, he could not bear to talk about it and many of Dickens's ideas about social conscience probably stem from this episode in his life.

Dickens taught himself shorthand and, by the age of sixteen, was working as a court reporter. This job allowed him to see, first hand, the harsh system of justice which then operated in England. Dickens tired of this dull work and became a newspaper reporter, commenting on Parliament. His newspaper work gave him a detailed knowledge of London and its inhabitants, both rich and poor, and he was to make use of this in many of his novels and stories.

Dickens became interested in literature and in 1832 he began writing sketches and stories about London life. These began to be published in 1833 and were published together in 1836 as *Sketches by Boz*. This sold so well that Dickens was asked to write some more sketches. This project developed into *The Posthumous Papers of the Pickwick Club*, which appeared as a monthly serial. This form of serial publication was used a great deal by Dickens.

Charles Dickens never forgot his early brush with English justice and many of his works deal with the problems of growing up in poverty.

Dickens's success on both sides of the Atlantic led to a series of public reading tours.

He became a very successful author and was famous in both England and America. When the episodes of *Oliver Twist* surrounding the death of Nancy were published there were crowds on the dockside in New York, eagerly wanting to buy the latest instalment. Dickens also gave public readings from his works and these were hugely popular. His wealth allowed him to buy a large house, Gad's Hill, outside London, near countryside like that described in the opening section of *Great Expectations*.

The pressures of touring and the strain of putting great efforts into his public readings began to tell on Dickens and his doctors warned him to stop. He ignored their advice and his health deteriorated. He died in 1870, following a collapse at Gad's Hill.

Charles Dickens was born into times that saw great changes in the ways that people lived. The population still lived mainly in the countryside, but the industrial revolution, which had been underway for about sixty years, led to the rapid growth of cities. The growth was so rapid that the housing available to the poor was often appalling. Whilst many people worked long hours in dangerous factories and then went home to squalor, the wealthy few percent of the population lived in luxury.

A similar situation had led to revolution in France in 1789. Britain and much of Europe had been at war with the armies of revolutionary France for 19 years when Charles Dickens was born, and this war was to rage for a further three years until the defeat of Napoleon at Waterloo in 1815. The British government feared revolution at home and so maintained a very harsh regime. The army was called in to deal with any public gatherings which might become unruly. People could be imprisoned without trial. Public executions and transportation to the colonies were used extensively.

The law was a harsh and brutal instrument in the early nineteenth century.

The sentence of banishment from England had been introduced as early as 1597. After the loss of the American colonies in 1788, Australia was used as the main destination for convicts sentenced to transportation. Most of those transported were poor, uneducated people accused of theft. Between 1788 and 1868, 162,000 convicts (137,000 male, 25,000 female) were transported, mainly to New South Wales. Those who suffered this punishment were never meant to return home. Perhaps the most famous transportees were seven farm labourers form the Dorset village of Tolpuddle who were sentenced in 1834 for trying to organise trade union activities.

The 1800s were years of great prosperity for some in Britain. The new wealth generated by industry and the colonies was shared out amongst a privileged few. The gap between the rich and the poor grew and there were effectively two nations living in Britain. Those who had money made more and passed it on to their heirs; those who had no money were severely repressed and prevented from bettering themselves. Many people felt that a person was born to a particular station in society and could not move up the social scale.

Charles Dickens was very interested in bringing about change and his novels dealt with such topics as justice and punishment (e.g. *Oliver Twist*, *Great Expectations*), the harsh treatment of children (e.g. *Nicholas Nickleby*) and the evils of the factory system (e.g. *Hard Times*).

Dickens's own experiences had made him sensitive to poverty and injustice.

He campaigned long and hard against public executions, using his fame to bring the horrors of the situation to light. The campaigning of Charles Dickens and others led to the abolition of such executions. Hangings still took place, but behind prison walls.

Social change did come about during the lifetime of Charles Dickens. New laws were passed to curb the terribly long hours that factory workers had to endure. Young children were prevented from working in factories altogether. The Public Health Act of 1848 began the move towards improved sanitation.

Charles Dickens was an influential voice for 35 years and saw some of his ideas about social reform put into practice.

SUMMARIES

GENERAL SUMMARY

Part One

Pip, a young boy of eight or nine, meets a convict in the churchyard near the boy's home on the Thames marshes. Pip says that he lives with his sister and her husband, who is the local blacksmith. The convict is in irons and is hungry and so he makes the boy bring him a file and some food. Pip steals the items and takes them to the convict who then disappears. As the food is missed from the house, soldiers looking for two escaped convicts arrive and seek the help of Joe, the blacksmith. Out on the marshes they track Pip's convict who is found fighting with another escaped prisoner and is so determined not to let the other prisoner go that both men end up being caught.

Pip is sent for to go and play at a large house in the town. He finds the house is called Satis House and that it has a very strange inhabitant called Miss Havisham. She is an old woman who spends her days dressed in a faded wedding dress and surrounded by other decaying wedding items. The rooms she occupies have not seen daylight for many years and neither has she. There is also Estella, a girl of around Pip's age, whom Miss Havisham asks to play cards with Pip. Estella delights in humiliating the boy, but he finds her beautiful anyway.

A strange visitor to town gives Pip two pound notes and the man clearly has some connection with Pip's convict as he stirs his drink with the same file Pip had stolen. Pip meets the Pockets at Miss Havisham's and a strange boy makes Pip fight with him. Miss Havisham pays Joe to take Pip on as his apprentice and so he is sworn to the trade of blacksmith. In the meantime, Pip attends a poorly run night class in the town where he meets Biddy, a bright girl of a similar age to himself. Pip is not satisfied with his position in life and feels that he should be destined for greater things than being a blacksmith. Pip's sister is attacked and injured so severely that she can no longer speak. Pip suspects Orlick, Joe's assistant, who had argued with his sister earlier the same day.

A stranger arrives from London and announces himself as Mr Jaggers, a lawyer. Pip has seen him before at Satis House. He tells Pip that the boy is to inherit a large property and that he must go to London immediately to begin his training in life as a gentleman. As a condition, Pip is not to try to find out who his mysterious benefactor is. He assumes that it is Miss Havisham. Pip goes to London, leaving Joe and Biddy behind.

Part Two

In London, Pip begins his education with Mr Matthew Pocket, a cousin of Miss Havisham, and strikes up a close and lasting friendship with his son Herbert. He shares rooms with Herbert at Barnard's Inn.

Pip learns that his guardian, Jaggers, inspires fear and respect amongst the criminal community. He is a cautious and clever lawyer who is always on his guard. However, Pip becomes friendly with Wemmick, the lawyer's clerk, and pays some pleasant visits to his quaint home in Walworth.

During the next few years Pip learns how to spend money and gets into debt but he secretly arranges to help his friend Herbert in his career. His belief that he is being educated as a gentleman at Miss Havisham's expense so that he can marry Estella is strengthened when he is asked to accompany Estella in London. Estella tries to warn him that she has no feelings for him but he continues to hope.

Pip feels conscious that he has neglected Joe but he only goes to visit him to attend his sister's funeral. Joe's visit to Pip in London is an embarrassing occasion for them both.

One night Pip has a surprise visitor. It is the convict from the marshes, Abel Magwitch, who reveals that he is Pip's secret benefactor and he has returned illegally from Australia to see Pip. Pip is shocked, not least because this destroys his dream that he and Estella were destined to be married.

Part Three   Pip is horrified by the convict but feels bound to shelter him. He decides that, with Herbert's help, he will get Magwitch out of the country. Pip learns that the convict Magwitch fought with on the marshes, and who Magwitch blames for most of his troubles, is called Compeyson. This is the man who tricked Miss Havisham and failed to turn up to marry her.

Pip learns that Estella is to marry a surly, brutal man called Bentley Drummle, though he begs her not to throw herself away.

Wemmick warns Pip that he and Magwitch are being watched and the convict is lodged down the river, ready to catch a foreign steamer.

Gradually Pip pieces together the information that Magwitch is Estella's father and that her mother is Jaggers's servant, a woman he saved from the gallows. Estella had been given to Miss Havisham as her adopted daughter.

After regretting her past mistakes and helping Pip to finance Herbert in business, Miss Havisham is burned and later dies from her injuries.

Pip is lured down to the marshes by Orlick, who admits he attacked Pip's sister and who almost succeeds in murdering Pip. Luckily, Herbert comes to the rescue.

As Pip and Magwitch attempt to catch a ship, they are caught by the police. In the struggle, the police informant, Compeyson, is drowned. Magwitch who is injured, is tried and sentenced to death for returning to England. Magwitch dies before the sentence is carried out but not before Pip is able to tell him that his daughter is a beautiful lady and that he, Pip, loves her.

After Magwitch's death, Pip falls ill and is nursed by Joe. When he is well, he decides to go home and ask Biddy to marry him. He arrives to find it is Joe and Biddy's wedding day.

Pip accepts Herbert's offer of a job with his firm in Cairo. He returns after eleven years and accidentally meets Estella in the grounds of Satis House. She is now a widow. Pip feels sure that they will never part again.

PART ONE

CHAPTERS 1–3

Pip is an orphan and is living with his sister, Mrs Joe Gargery. She has married a blacksmith and the three of them live on the Thames marshes. The marshes are bleak and largely uninhabited. His parents and his five brothers are buried in the local churchyard and Pip often visits their graves. It is on one such visit to the churchyard that Pip is surprised by the convict.

Though frightening to Pip, the convict's actions can be seen as quite amusing.

A large frightening man seizes hold of Pip, threatens to cut his throat and turns him upside down in order to empty Pip's pockets. The man has irons on his leg and is very nervous. When Pip says that his mother is nearby the convict panics and starts to run. Pip actually means that his mother is buried nearby. The convict learns that Pip lives with a blacksmith and demands a file, so that he can free his legs, and food, which he calls wittles.

The convict threatens Pip by telling him that he has a wicked young man with him who will find Pip and cut his liver out if he informs anyone about whom he has just seen.

Mrs Joe is proud of the harsh way she has brought Pip up.

Pip returns home to his sister and Joe. She has an exaggerated view of the role she has played in his upbringing. She is a fierce, violent woman who beats Pip and intimidates her husband.

At the table, Pip hides his slice of bread in his trousers so that he can take it to the convict and keep his promise. The sound of large guns being fired makes Pip ask questions about the prison ships known as the hulks. The guns are fired when a prisoner escapes and Pip spends a restless night worrying that the young man is going to sneak into his bedroom and kill him.

Pip steals food from the pantry and sets off across the marshes to give it to the convict. He comes upon a man dressed like the convict from the graveyard and with an iron on his leg.

There are two convicts on the marshes after all.

Pip approaches the man from behind and is startled to find that this man is not the one to whom he is taking the food. The man tries to hit Pip but he manages to run away. At the old gun battery Pip meets the first convict and gives him the food. The convict is ravenous and eats the food so quickly that it astonishes Pip. When Pip says that he has seen the young man, the convict is amused that his story had been believed. When Pip goes on to describe him however, the convict becomes very anxious and says that he will 'pull him down, like a bloodhound'.

COMMENT

Pip's ideas about his brothers are touching and naive.

The marshes take on a threatening appearance after Pip has met the convict. His experience has changed the way he sees the world around him.

CONVICTS AT LARGE

Though the convict is a powerfully built man, he does not hurt Pip.

We are not given the name of Mrs Joe. This tends to make her a more distant character.

Joe Gargery is a blacksmith, yet he is bullied by his wife. This adds humour to the story.

There is clearly a second escaped convict on the marshes. The first convict has some reason to want to hunt this man down. This helps to establish the plot of Magwitch and Compeyson.

GLOSSARY

wittles victuals, meaning food

gibbet a frame on which the corpse of an executed prisoner would be displayed

plaister a poultice, wrapped round a wound to heal it

Tar-water a strong, black liquid made from pine bark

CHAPTERS 4–6

Pip explains his absence from the house on Christmas morning by saying that he has been to hear the carols. Joe and Pip go to church and Pip wants to tell someone what he has done. Some visitors arrive for dinner: Mr Wopsle, the clerk at the church, Mr and Mrs Hubble and Uncle Pumblechook, Joe's uncle.

Mrs Joe behaves differently in front of the guests.

Uncle Pumblechook has brought a bottle of sherry and a bottle of port for Mrs Joe. This is a tradition, as is Mrs Joe's pretence that the house is always this cheerful. Over the meal, Pumblechook, Wopsle and Mrs Joe discuss the ingratitude of the young and compare children to pigs. Wopsle continually interrupts Pumblechook. At the end of the meal, Mrs Joe offers Pumblechook some brandy. Pip is terrified as he took some of the brandy to the convict and added water to

Pip really thinks that he might be caught and Charles Dickens uses this to develop tension.

the remainder. Pumblechook drinks the brandy and immediately runs out of the door and coughs and charges round. Pip had not added water to the brandy, but Tar-water. There is nearly another calamity when Mrs Joe offers the guests some savoury pork pie; Pip had taken this to the convict, but he is saved by the arrival of a squad of soldiers who command everyone's attention.

The sergeant is carrying handcuffs which Pip thinks are for him. In fact, the handcuffs need repair and so the soldiers have come to the blacksmith. The sergeant announces that there are two escaped convicts on the marshes and that the soldiers expect to catch them at nightfall. Mr Pumblechook and the sergeant drink the wine that was supposed to be for Mrs Joe, then the soldiers leave to look for the escaped prisoners. Pip, Joe and Mr Wopsle accompany them. They follow the sound of shouting until they find two men fighting in a ditch. One is clearly stopping the other from running away, even though this means that both men will be caught. The man Pip describes as 'my convict' describes the other man as a villain and is pleased that this villain has been recaptured. He also says that he stole a pie and some other food from the blacksmith's house, thus preventing suspicion from falling on Pip.

Pip's conscience bothers him, but he still does not tell Joe what has happened.

COMMENT   Pip has a strong sense of right and wrong.

Mrs Joe becomes an even less sympathetic character in Chapter 4. She is mean and hypocritical.

Pip is troubled by not being able to own up to Joe and would like to confess in church, but there is no opportunity as it is Christmas Day.

There is no mention of a Christmas present for Pip. He is barely allowed to be a child in Mrs Joe's house.

Pip thinks that the handcuffs are for him. This adds a touch of humour and shows his naïvety.

The link between the two convicts is very strong, but unexplained. This hints at the reappearance of this plot strand later in the novel.

GLOSSARY   **Accoucheur Policeman** a midwife
            corn-chandler corn merchant
            omnipotent all powerful
            parley talk, conversation

CHAPTERS 7–8

Pip is not a natural scholar, but he is eager to learn.

Twelve months have passed since the episode with the convicts. Pip is to be apprenticed to Joe when he is old enough. He attends an evening school in the village, run by Mr Wopsle's great-aunt. She sleeps through the lessons and Pip has largely to teach himself to read, write and do simple sums. He writes a letter, in very basic English, to Joe. This leads to Joe telling Pip of his own difficult childhood with a drunken father who beat Joe and his mother. It is because of this experience that Joe is so tolerant of his wife. He does not want to find himself behaving like his own father had done. Pip admires Joe for this and finds himself looking up to the blacksmith from this point onwards.

Mrs Joe arrives back from market where she has been assisting Pumblechook. She announces that the rich, reclusive Miss Havisham has asked for Pip to go and play at her house. Pumblechook had suggested him to Miss Havisham when she had made enquiries to find a boy who would go and play there. Pip is scrubbed down and sent off with Pumblechook who is to take him to Miss Havisham the following morning.

Pip is taken to the run-down house of Miss Havisham and meets Estella for the first time. Pumblechook is peeved that he is not invited into the house with Pip. Estella tells Pip that the house is called 'Satis', meaning enough. She leads him by candlelight to the room in which Miss Havisham sits. Miss Havisham is dressed as a bride but everything in the room has aged and faded, including her. All watches and clocks in the room are stopped at twenty minutes to nine.

Miss Havisham is dressed as for her own wedding which should have taken place many years ago.

Miss Havisham tells Pip to play and, when he finds this difficult to do in such gloomy surroundings, Estella is sent for. She plays cards with Pip and humiliates him repeatedly, commenting that he is common as he calls knaves, jacks. Pip is told to come back in six days time and gets to explore some of the grounds of the house before Estella shows him out. She is happy that she is able to make him cry and Pip feels ignorant and resents his simple upbringing.

Estella is cruel, but she is also lonely herself. The bitterness of Miss Havisham seems to have affected her.

COMMENT

Learning to read and write does not come easily to Pip, and he receives no help from home.

Pip is proud of the letter and Joe is delighted with it, though the only part he can read is his own first name.

Joe does not condemn his father for the years of brutality, but insists that the man had a good 'hart'. This shows Joe to be a very tolerant and forgiving man.

Pip has not actually been asked whether he would like to go to Miss Havisham's at all.

Pip is captivated by Estella's beauty but does not know how to handle the cruelty she shows him.

Miss Havisham is a pathetic character who has withdrawn from the world.

GLOSSARY   **erudition** hard study

Mo-gul a tyrannical Indian prince

like a young penitent into sackcloth like a pilgrim who wears
rough clothes to show he is humble

farinaceous floury

capricious acting on a whim

violent coercion being made to do something by force

CHAPTERS 9–10

Pip does not want his sister or Pumblechook to know the truth as they constantly bully him.

Pip is concerned that if he says what Miss Havisham and the house are really like, people will form the wrong impression. He is bullied by Mrs Joe and Pumblechook and so decides to invent an elaborate story about his visit. He says that:

- Miss Havisham is very tall and dark
- She was sitting in a black velvet coach
- Estella handed in wine and cake from a golden plate
- Four huge dogs ate veal cutlets from a silver basket
- They had all played with flags and swords
- There was a cupboard containing swords, pistols, jam and pills

Later, Pip admits to Joe that he had been lying and Joe scolds him, but reassures the boy that he is not ignorant and backward, as Estella had said, but a great scholar.

Estella has made Pip feel he is common; he decides to acquire an education.

Pip asks Biddy if she will teach him when he goes to the evening school and she agrees. On the way home, Pip calls at the Three Jolly Bargemen to collect Joe. There is a stranger in the pub who takes an interest in Pip. He appears to know about the episode with the convict on the marshes and reveals this to Pip by stirring his drink with the file that had been given to the convict a year earlier. The stranger gives Pip some money, which turns out to be the grand sum of two pounds. When he gets home and realises he has been given so much, Pip tries to return the money. When he returns to the Three Jolly Bargemen, the man has gone. The two pound notes are wrapped up and kept safe.

COMMENT Pip feels protective towards Miss Havisham and Estella, even though they are quite harsh with him.

His list of items in the cupboard is ridiculous and shows that his imagination is running away with him.

Pip is happy to lie to Mrs Joe and Pumblechook, but has to tell the truth to Joe.

The mysterious stranger and his gift must have some significance. Pip feels that there is a link with his convict.

Instead of rejecting the strangers at Satis House, Pip shows an affinity for them and is happy to distance himself from those who have bullied him for most of his life.

GLOSSARY **farden** farthing, a small coin, one quarter of a penny
sedan-chair a carriage that is carried on poles; the very rich would have used one
penitence regret
binding me apprentice apprentices would be bound to their masters for up to seven years whilst they learned a trade
metaphysics a branch of philosophy dealing with unknown forces

CHAPTER 11

Pip makes his second visit to Satis House. Estella shows him to a different part of the house where he is made to wait in a room which already has four people in it. – Sarah Pocket, Camilla and her husband, cousin Raymond, and Georgiana.

PIP MEETS THE POCKETS

The reader is left to puzzle out who these characters are in the same way that Pip is.

They are talking about someone called Tom and someone called Matthew, whose behaviour they do not approve of. Estella knows these people and the intrigue behind their visit. She leads Pip to Miss Havisham's room and taunts him on the way. She makes Pip say that she is pretty and then insults him.

This man's striking physical appearance is described carefully so that we will recognise him later.

A burly man passes Pip on the stairs and Pip reveals that this man is to be important to him later on. Miss Havisham leads Pip into a different room to that of his first visit. It is a large room with a very long table in it. On the table are the remnants of a wedding cake, covered in cobwebs and infested with spiders. Pip is made to walk Miss Havisham round the room and then to call for Estella. She arrives with the four visitors who take it in turn to flatter Miss Havisham:

The visitors do not dare to contradict their host, even when this makes them look foolish.

- Sarah Pocket says Miss Havisham looks well
- Camilla complains of her infirmities and says she lies awake at night thinking of Miss Havisham
- Raymond adds that his wife's worries about family troubles are making one of her legs shorter than the other
- Georgiana tries to be the last to say goodbye but is beaten in this by Sarah Pocket

Matthew seems dear to Miss Havisham yet he never visits her.

They discuss Matthew again. Apparently he refuses to visit. Miss Havisham is sure that he will come to see her when she is dead and laid out on the long table. The visitors have come to see Miss Havisham because it is her birthday. She does not celebrate it and does not even want it to be mentioned. Miss Havisham talks of a *he* who will be cursed when she dies, but she does not explain who this *he* actually is. Pip is then made to play cards with Estella, who treats him with scorn, though she does not actually insult him this time.

The boxing match is a good example of Charles Dickens's use of eccentric behaviour to create humour.

Pip explores the run-down grounds of the house and meets a boy of his own age (Herbert Pocket) who insists that they should fight. A boxing match takes place and Pip easily beats the other boy, who keeps on fighting until he has been almost knocked out. Estella seems to have been watching and she appears to be pleased with Pip, so much so that she lets him kiss her on the cheek as he leaves.

COMMENT

Charles Dickens introduces a new element to the plot, the Pocket family, and links it to the strange behaviour of Miss Havisham. This develops intrigue.

The visitors attempt to outdo one another in their efforts to impress Miss Havisham.

Estella is vain and is encouraged in this by Miss Havisham. She is also lonely and used to amusing herself.

The room has decayed as much as has Miss Havisham and she affects the whole environment of the house.

Miss Havisham was to have been married on her birthday. The coincidence of these two supposedly happy days creates more pathos (see Literary Terms) when we see what she has become.

GLOSSARY

toadies and humbugs miserable people, the equivalent of 'creeps'

trimmings to their mourning items of sombre clothing worn out of respect for a recently deceased person

epergne a fancy cake stand

nicety exactness

PIP IS APPRENTICED

CHAPTERS 12–14

Pip is worried about having hurt the boy with whom he had fought at Miss Havisham's. He returns nervously to the house and pushes Miss Havisham in her chair. He continues to call every other day at noon for eight to ten months. Miss Havisham asks him what he is going to be and Pip tells her of the plans for him to be apprenticed to Joe.

Miss Havisham helps Pip but she is also prepared to allow him to be humiliated as practice for Estella.

Estella continues to treat Pip with disdain, though sometimes she is quite friendly towards him which confuses him. Miss Havisham seems to take great delight in Estella's ability to captivate Pip and urges her to 'break their hearts and have no mercy!'.

Pumblechook insists on interfering in the plans for Pip's future and the boy becomes increasingly infuriated with him. Miss Havisham asks Pip to bring Joe to see her so that the matter of Pip's apprenticeship can be settled. Mrs Joe is incensed at the invitation to Joe as it excludes her.

Pip is starting to feel that his simple life with the blacksmith is now beneath him.

Joe and Pip visit Satis House and are shown in by Estella, who takes no notice of either of them. Throughout the conversation with Miss Havisham, Joe addresses Pip instead of her. This makes Pip feel ashamed of Joe. Miss Havisham gives the blacksmith twenty-five guineas to pay for Pip to be apprenticed to him and she makes Joe agree that he will not look for any more money from her. Pip is told that he is not to visit again.

Joe hands over the money to his wife and Pip is taken to the Town Hall to have his indentures sworn out. A party is held in Pip's honour, but by the end of it he feels that he will never settle to Joe's trade, even though he once dreamt of being a blacksmith.

Pip is not satisfied with his trade but he does not complain as he does not want to upset Joe. He thinks of Estella a great deal and wishes that he could see her again.

COMMENT   Estella is beautiful but cruel. She has been heavily influenced by the bitterness of Miss Havisham towards men.

The absurd conversation between Joe and Miss Havisham is typical of the way Charles Dickens creates humour through eccentric behaviour.

Miss Havisham does not need to make Joe promise not to seek anything else from her. She is being rather mean and suspicious.

Miss Havisham pays Joe in guineas, which had gone out of circulation in 1817. They were still legal tender but show Miss Havisham's old-fashioned ways.

Joe does not seem to realise the difference between pounds and guineas, possibly because he has never had so much money in his life before.

GLOSSARY   **incrimsoned countenance** face made red, in this case through fighting

suborned recruited

court-suit best suit

a pair of pattens wooden soles which were tied to the shoes to keep the wearer's feet dry

indentures a formal contract binding Pip to Joe as his apprentice

Collins's Ode *Ode on the Passions* by William Collins (1721–59)

CHAPTER **15**

Pip continues his education under Biddy and Wopsle,
but neither teaches him very much. Wopsle uses Pip as
an audience for his eccentric performances and
sermons. Pip feels that he should visit Miss Havisham
(and Estella) again, but Joe feels that she will think the
boy wants something from her.

Orlick is described
in an
unsympathetic
way. He is
constantly referred
to as 'slouching'.

Joe's assistant Orlick is introduced. He is a bad-
tempered man and resents Pip's appearance in the
forge. He says that his first name is Dolge, but Pip
thinks this unlikely. When Pip asks for a half-holiday,
Orlick insists that he should have one too. Joe agrees,
but his wife scolds him for being weak. This leads to an
argument between Orlick and Mrs Joe. Joe has to
intervene and he and Orlick fight; Joe wins easily. An
uneasy peace descends on the forge.

Pip visits Satis House where Sarah Pocket admits him
reluctantly. Miss Havisham tells Pip that Estella is
abroad, being educated. She takes a wicked satisfaction
from the fact that this news upsets Pip.

Orlick is
establishing his
alibi and putting
the blame onto an
escaped convict.

On the way home, Pip meets Wopsle and is persuaded
to join him and Pumblechook in reading the tragedy of
George Barnwell. They spend several hours doing this
and when they head home they come across Orlick who
is waiting beside the road. He says that he has been up
town and was not far behind the others. He points out
that the guns at the Hulks are firing again, showing
that a prisoner has escaped. When they pass the Three
Jolly Bargemen they hear that someone has entered the
house when Joe was out and that a person has been
attacked. They run to the house and Pip finds his sister
unconscious; she has been hit on the head while her
back was turned to the door.

y

COMMENT   The argument and the fight should put Orlick under suspicion for the attack on Mrs Joe. Notice that it is Orlick who mentions the guns firing from the Hulks. An escaped convict is good cover for an attack.

Miss Havisham is very cruel to Pip, even though his visit is purely out of friendship.

Keeping Pip at Pumblechook's allows Charles Dickens to have the attack on Mrs Joe take place without the boy's knowledge.

Orlick's sudden appearance by the roadside is very suspicious in the light of the earlier argument.

GLOSSARY   **the tragedy of George Barnwell** a popular play from the eighteenth century. Barnwell is persuaded by his lover to rob his master and kill his uncle. He and his lover are hanged

Keep in sunders keep apart, derived from the word asunder

journeyman a skilled or semi-skilled worker who worked for a skilled tradesman

Newgate a notorious London prison

CHAPTERS 16–17

The events surrounding the attack on Pip's sister are explained. Before nine o'clock, a farm labourer had seen her in the doorway of the kitchen. Joe was in the Three Jolly Bargemen at the time. When he returned home at five to ten he found his wife on the floor. The fire had not burnt down, but the candle had been blown out. She had been struck with something heavy on the head and the spine and then something heavy had been thrown down at her. On the ground beside her was found a convict's leg-iron which had been filed open. Joe announced that it had not been filed open recently. Pip is sure that it is his convict's iron, the one he supplied the file for.

Who could have placed the convict's leg-iron in the farmhouse?

THE ROUTINE OF THE FORGE

Pip suspects Orlick but he has made sure that he had been seen in town during the evening. The constables and the Bow Street detectives stay around the house for two weeks, accuse numerous innocent people and then leave. The culprit is not caught.

Mrs Joe never recovers from her injuries. She is left unable to speak and seems to understand little of what is said to her. Biddy joins the household on the death of her previous employer. Mrs Joe traces out what appears to be a capital letter T, which puzzles everyone. Pip eventually thinks it may be a drawing of a hammer and Biddy realises that it is meant to represent Orlick. She develops a fondness for Pip's company, which puzzles him.

This introduces the idea that Pip could become a gentleman.

Pip carries on his apprenticeship and visits Miss Havisham on his birthday. Pip notices that Biddy is growing into an attractive woman, but he is still preoccupied with Estella. Pip is still trying to learn to read and write, but Biddy picks up things much quicker than he does. Pip tells her that he wants to be a gentleman and wishes to lead a very different life. This disappoints Biddy. He tells her that he could not hope to win Estella if he were to remain common. He says that he wishes he could fall in love with Biddy but she tells him that he never will. Orlick has been paying Biddy some attention, but she hates him as much as Pip does.

COMMENT

The leg-iron mysteriously reappears and frightens Pip, as he is the only person who knows its history.

Though Mrs Joe had never got on with Orlick, it is him she sends for after she has been injured.

Pip notices that Satis House has not changed since the first time he visited it.

Pip is insensitive in the way in which he speaks to Biddy about Estella. Biddy would clearly like Pip to fall in love with her, but realises that he would never be satisfied.

GLOSSARY   **Bow Street Men** policemen from the main London police station in Bow Street

CHAPTERS **18–19**

Wopsle is not so clever as he thinks and the villagers see this for the first time.

Pip is in the fourth year of his apprenticeship. Wopsle is reading an account of a gruesome murder to a group of friends at the Three Jolly Bargemen. Pip and Joe are present. Wopsle is just about to declare that the accused is clearly guilty when he is interrupted by a stranger. This stranger is recognised by Pip as being the man who passed him on the stairs of Satis House. The man questions Wopsle's knowledge of the law and shows him up. He then asks to speak privately to Joe and Pip, whom he has been sent to seek out.

Pip jumps to the conclusion that Miss Havisham is preparing him to marry Estella.

The stranger introduces himself as Mr Jaggers, a lawyer from London. He tells Pip that the boy has great expectations and is to come into a 'handsome property'. The boy is told he must begin his education as a gentleman at once. Pip and Joe are astonished; Joe agrees to release the boy from his indentures. Jaggers says that there is one condition attached to the fortune that Pip is to inherit; he is not allowed to know the name of the person who is his benefactor. Pip is not even allowed to make the least enquiry as to his benefactor's identity. The boy is to keep the name of Pip.

Jaggers says that Pip must begin his education in London and that Matthew Pocket could be enlisted as a tutor. Pip recognises Matthew as the person who Miss Havisham thought would visit when she came to be laid out on the long table, dead. Pip tells Biddy of his new status and he is impatient to leave for London to begin his new life.

Pip handles the situation badly. He is already beginning to see himself as superior.

Pip tells Biddy he would like Joe to visit him in London, but that he is worried Joe might seem out of place. Biddy sharply points out that Joe is proud and

PIP IS TO BECOME A GENTLEMAN

Pip feels no shame over this, in fact he enjoys it.

would not want to be made a fool of. Pip visits Mr Trabb, the tailor, who fawns after the boy when he hears of his new wealth. Trabb's boy is humiliated by being made to run about after Pip who had been his equal until recently.

Compare this to the way Pumblechook used to speak to Pip when Mrs Joe was present.

Pip visits Pumblechook, who tries to take credit for setting Pip off on the road that led to his fortune. Pumblechook gives Pip fine food and wine and speaks to him like an old friend. He then suggests that Pip might like to invest in his corn business.

Because Miss Havisham knows Jaggers, Pip is sure that she is responsible for his great expectations.

On the final day, Pip dresses in his new suit and visits Satis House. Sarah Pocket admits him and he visits Miss Havisham as she is taking another of her walks around her candlelit room. He tells Miss Havisham of his good fortune and says he is grateful for it. She has already heard from Mr Jaggers and she questions Pip as to the name of the rich person who has adopted him. She finally comments that he will always keep the name of Pip.

Pip says goodbye to Joe and Biddy and takes the coach to London. Only then does he begin to think he might have behaved ungratefully to Joe.

COMMENT

Mr Jaggers shows that he is a very just man and impresses Pip with his integrity.

Pip is so wrapped up in himself that he never stops to consider the feelings of Joe or Biddy.

The introduction of the mysterious benefactor adds a new dimension to the story.

Pip does not see that Miss Havisham's recent treatment of him is totally at odds with her providing him with a fortune. He takes the 'handsome property' to mean Satis House.

The suggestion of Matthew Pocket as Pip's tutor
intrigues him, possibly as he thinks Matthew might
shed some light on the situation with Miss Havisham.

Pumblechook also assumes that Miss Havisham is Pip's
mysterious benefactor.

Pip thinks that Miss Havisham's questions are a trap
and they confirm for him that she is his benefactor. Her
final comment about his name reinforces this idea.

GLOSSARY   **Timon of Athens and Coriolanus** characters from Shakespeare;
                  Timon was very miserable and Coriolanus was very hot-
                  tempered
              fell pugilistic purpose fell means dreadful, pugilistic means
                  fighting with your fists
              finger-post a signpost like a finger pointing the way

A *Identify the speaker.*

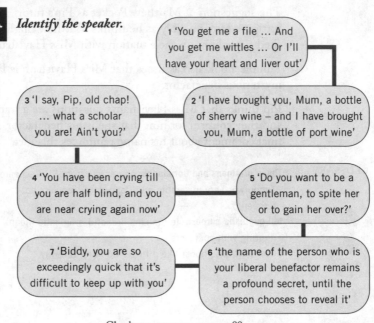

1 'You get me a file ... And you get me wittles ... Or I'll have your heart and liver out'

3 'I say, Pip, old chap! ... what a scholar you are! Ain't you?'

2 'I have brought you, Mum, a bottle of sherry wine – and I have brought you, Mum, a bottle of port wine'

4 'You have been crying till you are half blind, and you are near crying again now'

5 'Do you want to be a gentleman, to spite her or to gain her over?'

7 'Biddy, you are so exceedingly quick that it's difficult to keep up with you'

6 'the name of the person who is your liberal benefactor remains a profound secret, until the person chooses to reveal it'

Check your answers on page 89.

B *Consider these issues.*

a How Charles Dickens portrays the convict as a sympathetic character, even though he frightens Pip.

b How Pip's naïvety is used to bring humour to the novel.

c The way that Pumblechook and Mrs Joe treat Pip.

d How Estella is made to seem both cruel and pitiable.

e How Pip reacts to Miss Havisham after his first visit, including his lying about what he had seen.

f The way that the reader is led to believe that Miss Havisham may be Pip's mysterious benefactor.

g How Pip behaves ungratefully to Joe and Biddy when he hears of his new fortune.

h The way in which Charles Dickens establishes several major plots in the first part of the novel.

y

CHAPTERS 20–22

*Pip's first
impressions of
London are
coloured by the
gallows and the
criminal law
business.*

After a journey of five hours Pip arrives in London. He is impressed by its size and ugliness. A hackney coachman takes him to Mr Jaggers's office where a clerk tells him that the lawyer is in court. Pip is shown into Mr Jaggers's room to wait but he finds it very depressing, particularly as it contains two very ugly plaster casts of swollen faces. He decides to take a walk round the area and is disgusted by the blood and dirt of Smithfield meat market and horrified by the gatekeeper of Newgate prison who shows him the gallows.

Back at Jaggers's he finds that several other people are awaiting the lawyer's return. These turn out to be clients and Jaggers deals with them in a firm and sometimes brutal manner when he arrives. He rejects one client's bogus witness in disgust because his appearance is so awful.

When they are alone Jaggers tells Pip that he is sending him to stay at Barnard's Inn with young Mr Pocket until Monday when he will be taken to visit Mr Pocket's father to see if it suits him there. Mr Jaggers tells him about his allowance and the arrangements for credit with various tradesmen. He says he will try to keep Pip out of debt but no doubt Pip will go wrong somehow. The clerk, Wemmick, is told to take Pip to Barnard's Inn.

Pip talks to Wemmick on the way and thinks him to be a rather dry little man in appearance and manner. Wemmick is surprised when Pip offers to shake his hand on parting. He says he has got out of the habit.

Barnard's Inn is a shabby collection of buildings in a poor state of repair. Mr Pocket Junior's rooms are on the top floor and Pip finds a note saying that the occupant is out but will be back shortly. Pip is surprised

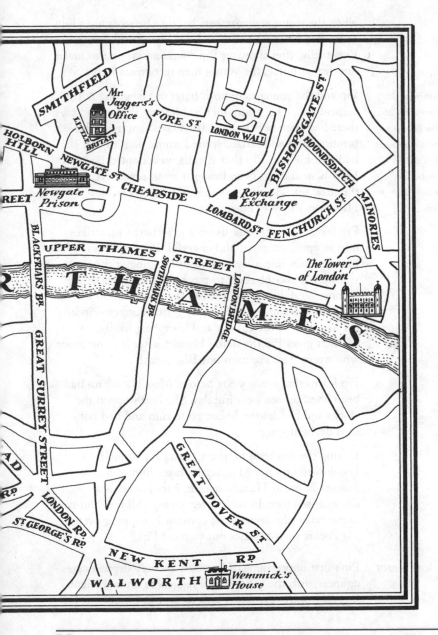

when the young man appears because he recognises him as the boy he fought with at Miss Havisham's house. Eventually, after showing Pip round and trying to make him feel at home, the young man recognises him.

Herbert is informative about Miss Havisham and his comments on Pip's table manners are amusing but gentle.

Pip and the young man both burst out laughing at the coincidence. The young man is Herbert Pocket and says there had been hopes that Miss Havisham might have favoured him and settled some fortune on him, but she had not. He tells Pip that Estella was adopted by Miss Havisham and has been brought up to exact revenge on the male sex. He also says that Mr Jaggers is Miss Havisham's man of business.

Pip takes an immediate liking to Herbert who strikes him as open, generous and cheerful. Pip confides in him and tells him all about his upbringing at the smithy. He asks Herbert to put him straight about manners and during their meal, the conversation is regularly interrupted as Herbert gently corrects Pip in his handling of the cutlery and his eating habits. Herbert gives Pip the name Handel, after the composer who wrote 'The Harmonious Blacksmith'.

Pip learns that many years before, Miss Havisham had been jilted on her wedding day. She had stopped the clocks and had let the house go to ruin and had not seen daylight since.

During the weekend Herbert shows Pip around London and on the Monday he takes him to his parents' house at Hammersmith. Mrs Pocket is a disorganised woman with seven young children and two nursemaids who seem to be constantly tripping over. Mr Pocket senior comes out to meet Pip.

COMMENT　Pip's first impressions of London are very depressing – ugliness, dirt, the gallows and Jaggers's criminal clients. Jaggers inspires great fear and respect in his clients. He is willing to use tricks like false witnesses but he is careful to keep himself in the clear.

Pip takes an immediate liking to Herbert and feels he can confide in him. We see that Herbert is a tactful and kind young man when he is correcting Pip's table manners.

The belief that Miss Havisham is his benefactor seems to be confirmed by the connection between her and Jaggers. Herbert seems to be of the same opinion.

GLOSSARY   **Smithfield** the wholesale meat market of London
half-a-crown a silver coin
portal gateway
farden farthing, a small coin, one quarter of a penny
frouzy frowzy, untidy, offensive
pottle a basket made from strips of interwoven wood
Tartar a fierce, frightening person

CHAPTERS 23–25

The Pocket household appears to be run by and for the servants. Mrs Pocket takes little notice of what goes on around her. She is greatly concerned with the fact that her father was nearly a member of the nobility. Mr Pocket, who is to be Pip's tutor, is a pleasant man whose patience is severely tested by the disorder in the household. He welcomes Pip and shows him to his room. He has two other boarding pupils Startop and Bentley Drummle. The evening meal is a chaotic affair disrupted by incidents involving the children and servants.

Pip settles in at the Pocket house but feels he would like to keep his room at Barnard's Inn and so be able to share his time between the two. He goes to see Mr Jaggers who provides him with money to buy furniture. Pip finds that Jaggers's way of dealing with him makes him uncomfortable but Wemmick reassures him that this is just his professional manner. Wemmick shows Pip round the premises and tells him that the two ugly plaster casts are death masks of ex-clients taken after they were hanged.

Wemmick invites Pip to visit his home at Walworth at some future date. He asks if Jaggers has invited Pip to dine with him yet and suggests that when he does Pip should take a look at his housekeeper. At Wemmick's suggestion they go to a police court to watch Mr Jaggers at work. Pip gets the impression that everyone there is terrified of Jaggers, even the magistrates.

At Hammersmith, Pip enjoys rowing on the river with Herbert and the other two pupils. He finds Drummle surly and proud and prefers the company of the more gentle Startop. Pip's education proceeds well but he is also learning how to spend money.

Wemmick becomes warm and human when he goes home to Walworth.

After a few weeks Pip writes to Wemmick and arranges to go home with him to Walworth one evening. They meet at Jaggers's office and make the journey on foot. When they reach Wemmick's house Pip is surprised to find that it is a little wooden building like a toy castle, complete with drawbridge, flagpole and a small cannon. Wemmick proudly informs Pip that this is all his own work. He asks Pip not to mention his home life to Jaggers as he likes to keep the office and the Castle separate.

Inside, Pip is introduced to Wemmick's elderly father who is extremely deaf. Pip is encouraged to please the old man by nodding his head frequently. At nine o'clock Wemmick goes out and fires the cannon, which delights his father, as it is the only sound he can hear. Pip stays the night and in the morning walks to Jaggers's office with Wemmick, noticing that Wemmick's manner becomes more stiff and hard the nearer he gets to his place of work.

COMMENT   Pip does not know how to deal with Jaggers but comes to realise that he has a formidable reputation in the criminal world.

We see the beginnings of Pip's extravagance with money.

The visit to Wemmick's home is a comic but touching episode. We see that Wemmick is a kindly and sensitive man when he is away from his depressing working environment.

GLOSSARY   **plebeian** low class
dower wedding gift
divers several, more than one
one of the elect one of the chosen, someone special
wherry small, light rowing boat
brazen bijou a small brass ornament or box
roasting-jack a device for roasting meat over the fire

CHAPTERS **26–28**

Jaggers invites Pip to dine with him the following evening and tells him to bring Herbert, Drummle and Startop. They all meet at the lawyer's office and Jaggers conducts them to his house in Soho which Pip finds to be a grim, dark building. Jaggers examines Pip's companions and at once takes a great interest in Drummle who he names the Spider. Pip takes the opportunity to observe Jaggers's housekeeper. She is a tall pale woman of about forty. She seems tense and always keeps her eyes on Jaggers.

Jaggers seems fascinated by the surly Drummle and christens him 'Spider'.

After Drummle has been boasting about his strength Jaggers makes his housekeeper show her wrists, much against her will. He tells them he has never known a stronger grip in man or woman. Drummle becomes increasingly rude and unpleasant. Jaggers appears to enjoy this but he eventually has to stop him from throwing a glass at Startop. Later he tells Pip that he likes the Spider but that Pip should stay clear of him. About a month later, Drummle finishes his tuition at Mr Pocket's and goes home.

Pip receives a letter from Biddy to say that Joe is coming to London with Mr Wopsle and would like to visit him. This is not welcome news as Pip has become ashamed of his background. Joe's visit is embarrassing and awkward as the blacksmith feels completely out of place. He is clumsy and confused and upsets Pip by calling him 'sir'. He delivers a message from Miss Havisham that Estella has come home and would like to see Pip. Joe refuses Pip's invitation to dinner and suggests that Pip would see him in a better light if he visited him at the forge.

The next day Pip sets out for home. At first he intends to stay with Joe and Biddy at the forge but he manages to convince himself that this would be an inconvenience to them and that he ought to stay at the Blue Boar. Two convicts are on the coach. They are being taken down to the prison ships off the marshes and Pip is *Pip has an*   horrified when he recognises one of them as the man *unpleasant*   who gave him two pound notes in the Three Jolly *reminder of the*   Bargemen one Saturday night. The convict does not *convict on the*   recognise Pip but Pip overhears him telling his *marshes.*   companion how another convict had asked him to give the two pounds to a boy who had fed him and kept his secret. Pip gets off the coach as soon as it reaches town and goes to the Blue Boar.

COMMENT   Pip is impressed by Jaggers's fierce-looking housekeeper. Wemmick had described her as 'a wild beast tamed'.

Pip feels that Jaggers has a talent for discovering the worst sides of people's characters.

Pip has become a snob and a self-deceiver. Even though Joe's discomfort is comical, his simple dignity is a reproach to Pip.

Pip seems to be haunted by his background. The convict on the coach makes him realise how easily he could be exposed.

GLOSSARY   **breaking wittles** breaking bread, sharing a meal

shay-cart chaise, a light open carriage

do comb my 'air the wrong way irritates me, rubs me up the wrong way

bludgeon a heavy stick or club

choleric angry, red-faced

CHAPTERS 29–31

In the morning, Pip goes to Miss Havisham's house and is unpleasantly surprised to find that Orlick is employed there as gatekeeper. Sarah Pocket is also at the house. When Pip goes into Miss Havisham's room he does not immediately recognise the elegant lady who is sitting next to her. When she looks at him he realises that it is Estella and he finds her more beautiful than ever.

Miss Havisham encourages them to walk in the garden together and they talk of old times. Pip is puzzled by something that he sees in Estella but he cannot work out what it is. Estella warns Pip that she has no heart, no softness or sentiment but Pip is still convinced that Miss Havisham intends that they should be married. This is only strengthened later when Miss Havisham puts her arm round his neck and fiercely urges him to love Estella.

Despite all warnings, Pip's self-deception is complete.

Mr Jaggers arrives and both he and Pip are surprised to see each other. At dinner Jaggers is very quiet and avoids looking at Estella. It is arranged that Pip will meet Estella at the coach when she travels to London. Pip returns to the Blue Boar and thinks of Estella. He has not gone to visit Joe as he imagines Estella would not approve of him keeping up such lowly connections.

Next day Pip tells Jaggers of his misgivings about Orlick and Jaggers says he will sack him. Pip walks part of the way out of town so as to avoid meeting Pumblechook who has been telling everyone he is responsible for Pip's good fortune. He is mocked by the tailor's boy and is glad to get away and into the coach.

Back at Barnard's Inn, Pip tells Herbert about his love for Estella but Herbert says that he has known this all along. He, too, is of the opinion that Miss Havisham is Pip's benefactor, but he tries to warn Pip that

Y

In contrast with Pip, Herbert is in love with a girl of humble circumstances.

attachment to Estella may bring him unhappiness. He reminds Pip about her upbringing. Herbert confides to Pip that he is secretly engaged to a young woman called Clara who lives with her invalid father. He fears that his mother would not approve of the girl's social position and he is not yet in a position to marry and support a wife. Pip finds a playbill which Joe had given him. It advertises a performance of Hamlet starring Mr Wopsle and the two friends decide to go to it.

The performance of the play is incompetent and ridiculous. The actors are frequently interrupted and insulted by members of the audience. Mr Wopsle in the leading role is a particular victim of their low humour. Pip finds himself laughing despite feeling sorry for Wopsle. The friends try to leave quietly but are unable to avoid being taken to speak to the star who now calls himself Waldengarver. They are as polite about the play as they can be and out of pity they invite him home for supper.

COMMENT

Pip is still convinced that Miss Havisham has had him educated as a gentleman so that he can marry Estella.

Pip is warned by Estella and by Herbert that he may be bringing unhappiness on himself.

The description of the play in its detail and in the behaviour of the audience is a wonderful piece of comic writing.

GLOSSARY

rank dense, thick
purser an officer responsible for pay and provisions on a ship
truncheon a staff of authority, a sceptre

CHAPTERS 32–35

One day Pip receives a message from Estella. She is arriving in London the following day and requests Pip to meet her. Pip is at the coach office several hours early and while he is waiting he happens to meet Wemmick who is on his way to Newgate prison and he offers to show Pip round. Pip accepts and accompanies the clerk as he visits several of Jaggers's clients. After the visit he feels contaminated by the awful place and he walks around the area to free himself from its influence before meeting Estella.

When she arrives Estella seems more beautiful than ever. She behaves towards Pip with a strange mixture of friendliness and formality and reminds him that they are not free to do as they please. Pip is to take her to Richmond where she is to stay with a lady who is to introduce her into fashionable society. When she gives Pip her hand and he kisses it she reminds him of her warning about her lack of feeling but she allows him to kiss her cheek. Pip feels his love is hopeless but he cannot help himself.

Once again Pip is haunted by a sense of there being some strange connection between Estella and Jaggers.

On the way to Richmond they talk about Mr Jaggers and Pip experiences the same puzzling feeling he has had before in connection with Estella and Jaggers. Pip delivers Estella to Richmond and returns to the Pocket's house in Hammersmith.

Pip begins to have doubts about the benefits of his good fortune. He is troubled about his neglectful behaviour towards Joe and Biddy and he feels he has been leading Herbert into extravagance and debt. They have applied to join a drinking and dining club of which Bentley Drummle is a member and begin to keep late nights in an empty pursuit of pleasure. At times the two friends make futile attempts to organise

y

their finances. One evening, after going over the bills, Pip receives a letter with a black border which informs him that his sister has died and that her funeral will take place on the following Monday.

In his description of the funeral, Dickens shows us his skill in creating humour in tragic circumstances.

Pip believes that Orlick was responsible for his sister's injuries and is filled with anger but he knows he has no proof. The funeral is a grim farce organised by Trabb & Co. with professional mourners and lots of black crepe. Pumblechook and the Hubbles are in attendance. Joe says he would have preferred a more simple and homely burial but he thinks that this way shows more respect.

After the funeral Pip dines with Joe and Biddy at the forge and asks if he may stay the night in his old room. Pip is aware that Joe is not at ease in his company but he eventually relaxes afterwards when he smokes his pipe outside the forge. Later Pip talks to Biddy and learns that she intends to be a teacher now that her work at the forge is ended. They talk about Pip's sister and about Orlick who Biddy says she has seen lurking around. Pip says he intends to visit Joe often but is hurt when Biddy appears to doubt him. He still feels this sense of injustice in the morning when he says goodbye and promises Joe he will be back. However Biddy is quite justified in her doubts.

COMMENT

Pip still believes that there is a plan that he and Estella shall marry although he is hurt by her manner towards him. He still disregards her warnings.

Good fortune has not brought Pip happiness although he tries to convince himself he is having a good time.

When he stays the night at the forge Pip has a sense that he is doing Joe a favour and feels pleased with himself.

Biddy shows that she understands Pip better than he does himself when she doubts that he will return.

PIP COMES OF AGE AND HAS A SURPRISE VISITOR

GLOSSARY   **fetters** leg-irons for prisoners

frouzy frowsy, dusty, untidy

tumblers pigeons which can turn somersaults in the air

Coiner someone who makes counterfeit coins

pattens wooden shoes for keeping out of the mud

sable dressed in black

mummery foolish theatrical equipment

CHAPTERS 36–39

Pip and Herbert continue to run up debts. At last Pip reaches the age of twenty-one and, as he expected, he is summoned to Jaggers's office. Jaggers asks him if he knows how much he has been spending and Pip has to admit that he does not. Jaggers asks Pip if he has any questions for him. Pip asks him if he is to learn anything about his guardian but Jaggers will not give him any information on this topic. Pip then asks if he is to receive anything whereupon Jaggers produces a five hundred pound note and tells him that this is to be his annual allowance from this time forward until his benefactor appears and that he will be responsible for his own affairs.

Pip shows his generous nature in his desire to help Herbert in business.

Pip decides he would like to help Herbert to get a start in business and he asks Wemmick for his opinion. Wemmick tells him that his office opinion is that he may as well throw his money in the river but that if he wants to know his Walworth opinion he will have to call on him at home.

The following Sunday Pip goes down to Walworth and has tea with Wemmick, his father and Wemmick's friend, Miss Skiffins. Wemmick, when asked his advice about Herbert, says he will approach Miss Skiffins's brother with a view to finding Herbert an opening in business. Pip insists that this is to be done without Herbert's knowledge.

y

Gradually, with the help of Wemmick and Miss Skiffins's brother, Pip arranges an opening for Herbert with a young merchant. When Herbert arrives home with the news of his success Pip is moved to tears at the thought that his expectations have finally done someone some good.

Pip's thoughts are always turning to Estella and the house at Richmond where she is staying. His suffering is made worse because he knows that Estella only uses him to tease her other admirers when he goes to visit her. He experiences nothing but unhappiness in her company but he still dreams of being with her for the rest of his life. One day Estella tells him that Miss Havisham wants to see her and that Pip is to take her and bring her back.

At Satis House Pip is disturbed by the way in which Miss Havisham is eager to know all about the men who are fascinated by Estella. He still believes, however, that although Estella has been brought up to take revenge on men for Miss Havisham, it is still intended that she will marry him in the end.

We begin to see Miss Havisham as a pathetic figure as she begs for Estella's affection.

Pip witnesses a bitter quarrel between Miss Havisham and Estella. Miss Havisham complains that Estella never shows her any love or affection, that she is ungrateful. She becomes more and more emotional about this. Estella coolly replies that she is very grateful to her mother by adoption but that she cannot give her what she was never given herself. She is entirely Miss Havisham's creation. Pip spends a restless night at the house and at one point sees Miss Havisham wandering with a lighted candle moaning to herself.

Back in London, Pip and Herbert are at a meeting of the dining club when Pip takes great offence at Bentley Drummle's proposing a toast to Estella. Pip says that Drummle is lying when he claims to know her but

PIP COMES OF AGE AND HAS A SURPRISE VISITOR

Drummle is able to produce a note from Estella and
Pip has to apologise. It depresses him further to find
out that Drummle is pursuing her and is often in her
company. One night at a ball, Pip challenges Estella
about encouraging Drummle. Estella replies that she is
only deceiving Drummle as she does others. Pip is the
only one she does not deceive.

The description of
the foul weather
sets the scene for
the arrival of the
disturbing
visitors.

By the time Pip is twenty-three he and Herbert have
moved to apartments in the Temple. One stormy night
when Pip is on his own, as Herbert is abroad on
business, he hears a footstep on the stairs. When he
goes out with his reading lamp he finds a rough-
looking man of about sixty who seems to be pleased to
see him. Pip asks him his business and rather
reluctantly invites him in. Pip recognises him as the
convict from the graveyard on the marshes, the man for
whom he had stolen the food and the file. The man
kisses Pip's hands and goes to embrace him saying he
has never forgotten him.

Pip is shocked and horrified as the man gradually
discloses that he is his benefactor, that Jaggers is his
agent. After serving time in Australia, the convict had
made a great deal of money there and had rewarded Pip
by having him educated as a gentleman. He had
returned to England to see his creation even though he
would be liable to be hanged if he were caught in the
country. Pip finds him repulsive but shelters him and
gives him Herbert's bed. He then sits and thinks how
all his ideas about Miss Havisham's plans for Estella
and him were figments of his imagination and how he
has abandoned Joe for the sake of a convict. He feels
worthless.

COMMENT   Pip cannot get any helpful information from Jaggers about his benefactor.

It is to Pip's credit that he is determined that some good should come out of his good fortune. He secretly helps Herbert.

Deep down, Pip realises that the situation with Estella is hopeless but he cannot help himself and hangs on to the dream that they are intended to marry.

Miss Havisham begins to realise she has created something terrible in her training of Estella.

Drummle's pursuit of Estella is a further torture to Pip. He cannot bear to see her encourage the clumsy ill-tempered oaf.

When Pip discovers the real identity of his benefactor, he is faced with his own vanity and gullibility. His life has been guided by fantasy.

GLOSSARY   **apoplectic** as if in a fit, a sudden loss of movement
Wine-Coopering the manufacture of wine barrels
roll list
warmint varmint, a troublesome person

A *Identify the speaker.*

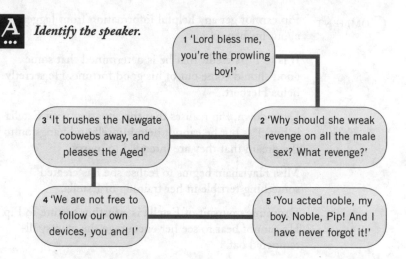

1 'Lord bless me, you're the prowling boy!'

3 'It brushes the Newgate cobwebs away, and pleases the Aged'

2 'Why should she wreak revenge on all the male sex? What revenge?'

4 'We are not free to follow our own devices, you and I'

5 'You acted noble, my boy. Noble, Pip! And I have never forgot it!'

Identify the person 'to whom' this comment refers.

6 'you'll see a wild beast tamed'

7 'The blotchy, sprawly, sulky fellow'

Check your answers on page 89.

B *Consider these issues.*

a Pip's first impressions of London.

b Your impressions of Mr Jaggers's law business.

c How Charles Dickens establishes Herbert's character.

d The factors which encourage Pip to believe Miss Havisham is his benefactor.

e The changes in Pip's character as he becomes a gentleman.

f How Charles Dickens makes Pip's visit to Wemmick's house humorous.

CHAPTERS 40–42

Pip decides to tell his cleaners and the gatekeeper that the convict is his uncle. He is disturbed to find that someone has possibly followed the old man into the building. Next morning the convict tells Pip something of his background. His name is Abel Magwitch but he is going under the name of Provis. He is proud of having created such a fine gentleman in Pip and he wants to see him spend his money.

When Pip goes out to order Magwitch some clothes he calls on Jaggers who confirms that the convict is indeed his benefactor. Jaggers is very careful not to acknowledge that Magwitch is in the country.

Magwitch's behaviour is threatening but there is a comical side to it.

No matter how he is dressed Magwitch seems to look like a convict in Pip's eyes. Pip is weighed down with dread of the man and the responsibility of protecting him. When Herbert returns he is surprised and shocked by Pip's guest and the news he has brought. Magwitch makes him swear on the Bible to keep his presence secret.

Pip has arranged lodgings for Magwitch nearby and after he has taken him round there, he and Herbert discuss what is to be done. They agree that the most important thing is to get Magwitch out of the country. Pip feels that he cannot take any more of Magwitch's money and that his presence in England is a danger to them all, however he feels bound to save the convict on account of the risks he has taken to see him. He realises that Magwitch will not leave the country without him so he resolves to go with him. Herbert agrees to help.

Next day Pip asks Magwitch about the fight with the other convict on the marshes and Magwitch tells the two friends his story. He says he has been in and out of jails all his life and does not remember his parents. Twenty years previously he had become involved with a

Most of the blame fell on Magwitch. Compeyson seemed such a gentleman. man called Compeyson, a swindler and forger who had been brought up as a gentleman. He became Compeyson's accomplice and when they were eventually caught, Compeyson saw to it that most of the blame fell on Magwitch who received a greater prison sentence. When Magwitch had been free on the marshes and had learned that Compeyson had also escaped he felt that the greatest revenge he could have would be to return Compeyson to captivity. However, Compeyson's punishment for escaping was light while Magwitch was transported for life. Herbert informs Pip that Compeyson was the man who abandoned Miss Havisham on their wedding day.

COMMENT   Pip's worries about Magwitch being discovered give him no time to dwell on his other problems.

Pip finds Magwitch repulsive and he wonders what sorts of crimes he may have committed.

Herbert is as loyal and dependable as ever. He agrees to help Pip without hesitation.

Magwitch's story is of a sad, pathetic and brutal life. He sees in Pip something good which he has managed to create.

GLOSSARY   **dram** a small drink of alcohol
grubber eater
molloncolly melancholy, sad
his skirts the tails of his coat

CHAPTERS 43–45

The behaviour of Pip and Drummle as they defend their places in front of the fire is childish and comical.

Pip feels he must see Estella and Miss Havisham one last time before he leaves the country with Magwitch. When he goes to Richmond he finds that Estella has gone to Miss Havisham's. This puzzles Pip as it is the first time she has made such a visit without his company. Next day Pip follows her. When he arrives at the Blue Boar he finds Bentley Drummle. They are rude to each other and neither mentions Estella but he hears Drummle announcing that he is to dine with a young lady that evening. Pip sees a man in the inn yard who reminds him of Orlick.

At Satis House, Pip accuses Miss Havisham of allowing him to dwell in the mistaken belief that she was his benefactress just so that it would upset her greedy relatives. She admits to this. He asks her to continue with the help he has given Herbert as he will not be able to do so.

Pip tells Estella he loves her and has always believed that they were meant for each other. Estella tells him again that she has no feelings. When he says he has seen Drummle, Estella tells Pip that she and Drummle are to be married. Pip begs her not to throw herself away on such a stupid brute but she says the arrangements have been made and that she is unlikely to be a blessing to him. Pip is heartbroken and declares that he will never forget her. He gives a passionate account of his love for her. As he leaves he has the impression that Miss Havisham regrets what she has done to Estella.

Pip is so distraught that he walks all the way back to London. When he arrives at the gate of the Temple he is given a note from Wemmick telling him not to go home. Pip spends the night in a hotel but cannot sleep.

Wemmick is an important source of information.

In the morning he goes to see Wemmick at Walworth. Over breakfast Wemmick tells him that he heard some prison gossip about Magwitch's return from Australia and also that someone has been watching Pip and his benefactor. Pip also finds out from Wemmick that Compeyson is in London. Wemmick has informed Herbert of the danger and Herbert has arranged lodgings for Magwitch at the house near the river where his girlfriend Clara lives with her father. This will be convenient for secretly getting on board a ship when the time comes.

COMMENT   Once again Pip feels the sinister presence of Orlick. It is not the first time that a man in dust-coloured clothes is mentioned. This is how the gatekeeper described the man who had followed Magwitch into the Temple.

Pip achieves a certain dignity in his confrontation with Miss Havisham. He is able to think of others and enlists her help to further Herbert's career.

With Estella's announcement that she is to be married all of Pip's dreams are shattered.

The danger mounts for Pip and Magwitch with news that they are being watched and that Compeyson is in London.

GLOSSARY   **smeary** smudged
great-coats overcoats
wicket small gate or door

CHAPTERS 46–48

In the evening Pip goes down to Mill Pond Bank where Herbert has taken Magwitch and is introduced to Clara who looks after her bedridden bad-tempered father. Magwitch has been lodged at the top of the house where he has a good view of the river. Pip tells him about Wemmick's information but decides to say nothing about Compeyson in case Magwitch is tempted to go after him. The convict agrees to Pip's idea that they should get out of the country and is pleased when Herbert suggests that Pip should buy a boat to row on the river. If they are regularly seen on the water no one will notice when they come down to pick up Magwitch.

Dickens builds up the tension with Pip's sense of being watched and with the incident at the play.

Next day, Pip buys the boat and he and Herbert become familiar sights on the river, sometimes rowing as far as Mill Pond Bank and back. However Pip cannot get rid of the feeling he is being watched or forget his fears for the safety of Magwitch.

Several weeks pass in this way while Pip awaits more news from Wemmick. One evening Pip goes to see Mr Wopsle perform in a play. During the performance, in which Mr Wopsle seems to play only a small part, he notices the actor staring at him. After the play Wopsle tells him he was staring at the man behind Pip and he was sure it was one of the convicts who was fighting on the marshes all those years ago. When he questions him Pip realises that Wopsle must mean Compeyson. Back at the Temple, Pip tells Herbert and also writes a letter to Wemmick with this news and reminding him that they are waiting for his hint.

About a week after this Pip meets Jaggers in the street and is invited home to dine with him. Pip accepts when he hears that Wemmick is also invited. At dinner

HIDING BY THE RIVER

Once again Wemmick is a source of information.

Wemmick is very distant with Pip and does not show any of his Walworth personality. He hands Pip a note from Miss Havisham who would like to see him about the business matter he had mentioned to her. To Pip's discomfort Jaggers brings up the subject of Estella's marriage to Drummle and proposes a toast that she will get the better of him. Pip notices Jaggers's housekeeper Molly standing nervously by and realises who she reminds him of. He becomes convinced that she must be Estella's mother.

Pip walks part of the way home with Wemmick who quickly reverts to his Walworth personality. When he asks about Molly, Wemmick tells him that over twenty years previously Jaggers had defended her on a charge of strangling a woman. She was also said to have murdered her own child, a little girl of three years. After her release she had gone to work for Jaggers. Wemmick has nothing more to tell him and they go their separate ways.

COMMENT

Herbert's happy relationship with Clara is a contrast to Pip's unhappy love for Estella.

Pip feels a genuine concern for Magwitch who has risked so much for him. Pip's better qualities are emerging in his hardship and disappointment.

Compeyson's presence behind Pip at the play is particularly mysterious and sinister.

Pip has had strange feelings about Jaggers's house and Estella for some time and now he realises that Molly is the connection. Her eyes and certain mannerisms have brought him to the realisation that she is Estella's mother.

GLOSSARY

porter-pot a mug for porter, a dark ale

necromantic work a book of spells for consulting the spirits of the dead

CHAPTERS 49–52

Pip gains dignity in his forgiveness of Miss Havisham.

Pip goes to see Miss Havisham on the following day. He walks the last few miles as he wants to avoid meeting people. When he reaches Satis House he finds Miss Havisham sitting by the fire and looking very lonely. She is full of remorse for what she has done and feels that Pip must hate her for it. He explains how she can help Herbert and she signs a note for Jaggers to release the money. She wonders if some day Pip will be able to forgive her. He tries to reassure her about this and tells her it would be better to try to undo some of the harm she has done to Estella than to worry about the past. He learns that Estella is now married to Drummle. In answer to Pip's question Miss Havisham says she does not know anything about Estella's parents, only that Jaggers brought her to Satis House when she was two or three years old.

As he is walking through the garden and the brewery yard before leaving, Pip imagines he sees Miss Havisham hanging from a beam. He is so uneasy that he calls back to her room. She is sitting by the fire. Suddenly her clothes catch fire and Pip throws first his coat over her and then the table cloth from the rotting wedding feast. She is badly burned and when the doctor arrives she is laid out on the wedding-feast table. Pip has received burns to his hands and arms. As Pip leaves, she is still regretting the harm she has done.

Back in London, Herbert looks after Pip. They both know how important it is that his hands should heal quickly so that he can row the boat when needed. Herbert tells Pip of a conversation he has had with Magwitch. The convict has told him how a woman he was involved with had been charged with murder and had threatened to kill their child. Pip realises he has been talking about Estella's mother. Magwitch believes that the woman carried out her threat. Pip tells Herbert that he is sure that Magwitch is Estella's father.

Pip is determined to find out the truth about Estella and next morning he goes to confront Jaggers about the matter. He tells Jaggers about the fire and Miss Havisham's injuries. He hands over the note concerning Herbert's money and is given a cheque. Pip then tells Jaggers that he knows who Estella's mother is. Jaggers does not comment on this but he is obviously surprised when Pip declares that he believes Provis to be her father. This is news to Jaggers but he tries to avoid the subject by carrying on his business with Wemmick.

We are shown a different side of Jaggers's character here as he reveals his motives for saving Estella.

Pip appeals to his good nature to be frank with him. Eventually Jaggers admits in his cautious way that he had taken in the murderess as his housekeeper and had controlled her violent nature. He had also given up her daughter for adoption to save her from the fate of so many similar children he saw in the course of his business. Jaggers says that it can do nobody any good to reveal the truth now.

When Pip delivers the cheque to Herbert's employer and sees him established as a partner in the business, he feels it is the one good thing he has done since he was first told of his expectations.

One morning he receives a letter from Wemmick suggesting he makes a move in the next few days. Pip has not fully recovered from his burns and Herbert suggests they enlist the help of Pip's old fellow student, Startop, but to tell him as little as possible. Herbert and Pip look for a likely ship and decide upon a steamer bound for Hamburg. They will wait for this ship in some quiet place down river and row out to it so that Pip and Magwitch can get on board. They arrange to pick up Magwitch from his lodgings on Wednesday.

When Pip gets home he finds an anonymous letter. The writer says if he wants to find out more about Provis (Magwitch) he is to come down to the limekiln on the marshes alone. Pip has very little time to consider this, so he goes to catch the coach and leaves a note for Herbert saying that he has gone to see Miss Havisham. As he sets out for the limekiln after dining at an inn he realises he has lost the anonymous letter.

COMMENT Pip can only pity Miss Havisham, she is such a pathetic figure. He shows generosity in his forgiveness and courage in tackling the fire.

All the parts of Estella's mysterious background begin to come together.

Jaggers reluctantly reveals that he too has feelings when he talks about saving the child.

Pip realises he is not thinking clearly as he goes down to the marshes in response to the letter.

GLOSSARY **great-coat** an overcoat
a Thames waterman a boatman with a licence to work on that river
sluice-house a building next to a sluice or dam
limekiln a furnace where lime is produced

CHAPTERS 53–55

Pip knows the marshes well and has no difficulty in finding the limekiln. He goes into the sluice-house nearby and finds it deserted but there is a lighted candle on a table. Suddenly the candle is extinguished and he is attacked from behind. He is tied to a ladder against the wall and is in great pain because of his burns.

ESCAPE AND CAPTURE

When his attacker relights the candle Pip discovers it is
Orlick. Orlick tells him he intends to kill him. He has
always hated Pip and blames him for most of his
misfortunes. He boasts of attacking Pip's sister but says
it was Pip's fault for making him angry. He says he
knows about Provis (Magwitch) and the plan to get
him out of the country. He has been working with
Compeyson and says that Magwitch will be taken.

Orlick is about to kill Pip with a hammer when the
door bursts open and Pip is saved by Herbert, Startop
and the draper's boy from the town, who has led the
rescuers to the limekiln. In the struggle Orlick manages
to escape. Herbert tells Pip he had found the
anonymous letter on the floor of their lodgings and had
been worried enough to follow him.

*Magwitch is
strangely passive
during the journey
down river. Pip is
now the man of
action.*

Back in London, Pip tries to rest and prepare himself
for the escape attempt. On the Wednesday morning,
Pip, Herbert and Startop take their boat from the
Temple stairs and start rowing down river. They pick up
Magwitch at Mill Pond Bank and carry on
downstream. Magwitch is disguised as a river pilot. He
seems the calmest of the party.

After dark they stop at an inn on a deserted stretch of
the shore and they spend the night there. Pip is uneasy
and sees two men looking at their boat during the
night.

Next day, they row out on the river to await the
steamer. As the steamer approaches they are hailed
from another rowing boat and Magwitch is called upon
to surrender. When the other boat closes with them
there is a struggle and Magwitch unmasks a man who
is with the police. It is Compeyson. At that moment
they are run down by the steamer. Pip, Herbert and
Startop are pulled aboard the police galley but
Magwitch and the other man have disappeared.

y

Magwitch is later pulled from the river and manacled. He is badly injured and he tells Pip that he and Compeyson had gone under together but that he had let go of Compeyson and swum away. Pip stays with Magwitch as he is taken back to London and he promises not to leave him. Magwitch's trial for returning from transportation is set for a month's time.

One evening Herbert announces that he will soon be leaving to run his firm's branch in Cairo. He offers Pip a job as clerk with the prospects of promotion to partner. Pip says he has too much on his mind to consider it clearly.

Wemmick's little scheme to enroll Pip as his best man is endearingly humourous.

On the day he says goodbye to Herbert, Pip meets Wemmick who invites him to take a walk with him the following morning. This turns out to be the day of Wemmick's marriage to Miss Skiffins and Pip is enrolled as the best man. Afterwards, Wemmick asks Pip not to mention it at the office.

COMMENT

Orlick has been shadowing Pip for a long time. He has hated him and resented him all his life.

Pip is resigned to the idea of going abroad with Magwitch. He feels he owes it to him.

As it turns out, the friends have been under observation all the time. The police and Compeyson have been waiting for them to make their move.

Pip shows strong loyalty towards Magwitch and compassion for him. He feels it would be better for him to die of his injuries than to be tried and hanged.

Pip's generosity towards his friend has provided Pip with the possibility of a future career. He will not be entitled to any of Magwitch's money even if he wanted it.

The comic scene at the Walworth wedding provides a humorous contrast to the sad events in London.

GLOSSARY   **farden** farthing, a small copper coin, one quarter of a penny
                pea-coats sailor's thick coats
                colliers coal ships
                a tithe a tenth
                scullers rowers
                bandboxes hatboxes
                galley a large open rowing boat

CHAPTERS 56–59

During the next month, Pip visits Magwitch in the prison infirmary every day and sees him grow weaker. When Magwitch comes to trial, Pip is allowed to stand near the dock and hold his hand. The trial is a mere formality as it is obvious that Magwitch has committed the crime of returning. He is sentenced to death with thirty-one other prisoners on the last day of the Court Sessions.

Magwitch is too weak to stand as he is sentenced to death.

Pip cannot rest and writes appeals and petitions to the Home Secretary and other important people on Magwitch's behalf. He continues to visit Magwitch and

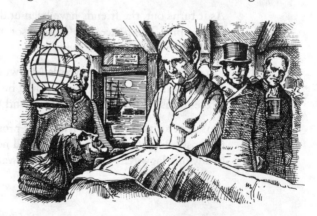

y

the convict's health steadily deteriorates. When he realises Magwitch is about to die he tells him that his daughter is alive and is now a fine lady and that he, Pip, loves her. Magwitch kisses Pip's hand before he dies.

Pip falls ill and is almost arrested for debt. For a while Pip is delirious and when he comes to his senses he finds that Joe has been looking after him. Someone had sent a letter informing Joe and Biddy of his illness. When Pip enquires about Miss Havisham, Joe tells him that she has died. Her property has been left to Estella apart from four thousand pounds to Matthew Pocket, Herbert's father, and some small amounts to other relatives. He also tells him that Orlick is in prison for robbing Pumblechook.

Joe's decency and simple dignity is still a bitter reproach to Pip.

Under Joe's care Pip gradually recovers. He tries to talk to Joe about his benefactor but Joe wants him to put the past behind him. As his health improves, Pip notices that Joe becomes more reserved with him and begins to call him 'sir' again. One morning he awakes to find that Joe has gone and has left him a note and a receipt for Pip's debt which he has paid off. Pip is determined to follow Joe and to tell him his true circumstances. He has also decided to ask Biddy to marry him.

Pip stays at the Blue Boar and in the morning he walks by Satis House and sees that the property is being prepared for an auction. When he returns to the inn for breakfast he finds Pumblechook who patronises him to such an extent that he quarrels with him. Pumblechook accuses him of being ungrateful to the man who was the cause of all his good fortune.

When he goes to the forge he is puzzled because he cannot hear the sound of Joe's hammer and the forge itself is closed. Then he discovers Joe and Biddy in their best clothes and they announce that they have just been

THE END OF MAGWITCH AND A NEW START FOR PIP

married. They are delighted to see him and Pip is only thankful that he had never mentioned to Joe his own thoughts of marrying Biddy. He congratulates them both and says he going abroad soon and will work to pay off the money he owes them. He asks their forgiveness for his past behaviour and goes to see his old room before he eats with them.

Within a month Pip leaves the country and goes to work for Herbert. He gets on steadily and is able to pay off his debts. Eventually he becomes a partner in the firm.

Eleven years later he returns to visit Joe and Biddy at the forge. Pip is delighted to find that they have a little boy who they have named after him. The following evening, thinking of Estella, he walks over to Satis House. He had heard that she had led an unhappy life with Drummle but that she was now a widow. The house and brewery have gone and only the old garden wall remains.

Estella appears almost like a ghost in the ruined grounds of Satis House.

As he is walking in the grounds he is surprised to meet Estella. She tells him that this is the first time she has been back. This piece of ground is all that remains of her property. She says she has often thought of Pip. She hopes they can still be friends even though they will be apart. Pip takes her hand and as they leave the garden he is convinced that there will be no more partings.

COMMENT

Pip shows great devotion to Magwitch in his final days. It redeems him in our eyes because he can gain no credit in polite society for being associated with a convict.

The mass sentence of death on thirty-two prisoners is a grim reminder of the legal system of the time.

It is a very moving scene when Pip tells the dying convict about his daughter. It is the final stage in our coming to look upon him as a sensitive and vulnerable human being.

Pip is deeply touched by Joe's care of him but as he recovers we see that the relationship between them has been changed for ever by Pip's becoming a 'gentleman'.

Pip is still taking things for granted when he assumes that Biddy will accept his proposal of marriage.

When they finally meet in the ruined garden of Satis House, both Estella and Pip have learned hard lessons from their experiences and are perhaps fit to make a future together.

GLOSSARY   **prison-breaker** escaper
             gewgaws showy things without value
             finger-post a signpost like a finger pointing the way

A *Identify the speaker.*

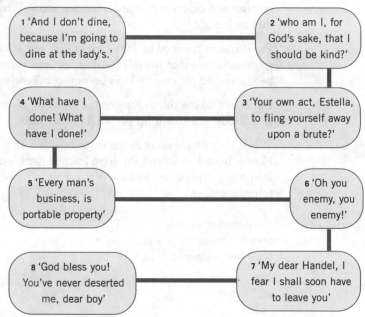

1 'And I don't dine, because I'm going to dine at the lady's.'

2 'who am I, for God's sake, that I should be kind?'

4 'What have I done! What have I done!'

3 'Your own act, Estella, to fling yourself away upon a brute?'

5 'Every man's business, is portable property'

6 'Oh you enemy, you enemy!'

8 'God bless you! You've never deserted me, dear boy'

7 'My dear Handel, I fear I shall soon have to leave you'

Check your answers on page 89.

B *Consider these issues.*

a How Pip's character changes in Part 3 of the novel.

b How Magwitch is presented.

c How the danger to Magwitch is built up.

d The changes in Miss Havisham's relationships with Pip and Estella in Part 3.

e How Pip and Herbert have helped each other.

COMMENTARY

THEMES

Self-knowledge

Self-knowledge or self-discovery is an important theme in the novel. Pip rejects his humble origins at the forge and aspires to become a gentleman. Although he is given material wealth and is taught table manners and how to speak in a different way, he loses much in the process. It is only through hardship, loss and the example of Joe that he comes to humbly realise the worthlessness of his previous behaviour and the emptiness of his ambitions. Joe does not change. He realises that he is in his element at the forge and he never loses his basic decency and honesty. Estella is aware of what she is doing but makes the mistake of thinking that she cannot be hurt by such a destructive way of life. Her experiences with Drummle and the passing of time bring her to realise what she lost when she rejected Pip's love.

Justice

There is an underlying theme of natural justice in the events of the story. Loyalty and goodness are rewarded. We feel that true and faithful Herbert deserves his happy marriage to Clara and that Joe and Biddy deserve their happiness together. We may also believe that Pip and Estella can be allowed a happy future when they have paid the price of their vanity and folly. Magwitch is an instrument of justice in his way. He tries to reward Pip for helping him on the marshes. He makes Compeyson pay the ultimate price for his past crimes, which the legal system had failed to do. The legal system itself is seen to be brutal, arbitrary, corrupt and open to manipulation by the likes of Jaggers. However Jaggers has tried to counter the effects of this system by saving one little girl, Estella, from its horrors.

Humanity	Human values are seen to prevail over wealth and position. Miss Havisham's wealth brings her no comfort at all. She uses it as a tool to upset her grasping relatives and to work her revenge on the male sex through Estella. Bentley Drummle has wealth but is a brutal and stupid bully, a worthless human being. Wemmick may talk about the importance of portable property but his greatest happiness lies in his warm human relationships and his simple pleasures in Walworth. Pip's wealth and position bring him no good at all except for the opportunity to help Herbert. The human values of Joe and the forge, of Wemmick's Walworth sentiments and of Herbert's love for Clara are those which bring happiness.
Pride and revenge	Pride and the desire for revenge are shown to be extremely destructive. Miss Havisham feeds these destructive forces by keeping around her the reminders of her humiliation and betrayal. Her life is distorted. She lives in the dark and she ruins the lives of Estella and Pip through her selfish obsession.

STRUCTURE

The novel was finally printed in the three 'stages' that it is printed in today, but it was first published in weekly instalments. This means that *Great Expectations* does not have the structure of a conventional novel. Instead of moving towards a general climax, the story has many mini-resolutions of the plot. Each new episode needed a cliffhanger type ending in order to ensure that the public would buy the next. This has often been seen as a weakness of Charles Dickens's novels as the story can become repetitive.

Great Expectations was originally published in the following instalments:

Part One	Chapters 1–2; 3–4; 5; 6–7; 8; 9–10; 11; 12–13; 14–15; 16–17; 18; 19
Part Two	Chapters 20–21; 22; 23–24; 25–26; 27–28; 29; 30–31; 32–33; 34–35; 36–37; 38; 39
Part Three	Chapters 40; 41–42; 43–44; 45–46; 47–48; 49–50; 51–52; 53; 54; 55–56; 57; 58; 59

Charles Dickens was persuaded to change the ending of the novel. Originally there was to be no Chapter 59. The novel was to have ended with Estella remarrying after Drummle's death. There was to have been a short meeting between Pip and Estella some years later but no future for the two as a couple. This ending was preferred by Dickens as he felt that it was more realistic than a romantic one. He changed his mind after visiting his friend and fellow novelist Sir Edward Bulwer-Lytton. Bulwer-Lytton thought that the original ending was too disappointing and Dickens quickly wrote the ending that has subsequently been used in all editions.

In *Great Expectations*, Charles Dickens tells the story through the character of Pip. This is not as simple as it may at first seem. The Pip that tells the story is an adult who is thinking back on his life. When we are given information about Pip's childhood we are given it by the adult Pip. This is very important. Consider the differences between these two possible accounts:

- A child's version of the first day at school
- An adult's story about a child's first day at school

The accounts are likely to be very different indeed. All of the incidents in the novel are told to us by the adult Pip.

PIP

Wants to be a gentleman
Blind obsession with Estella
Obtains humility

At the start of the novel, Pip is an innocent boy who has been brought up to respect his elders and betters. He is a kind-hearted child as is seen in the episode in which he brings the convict the file and the food. He is also rather gullible and really believes that a terrible man will tear his liver out while he sleeps unless he does as he has been told. This gullibility can be seen again when he visits Miss Havisham's house and is taken in by the charms of Estella.

Once he has met Estella he begins to change. Because she has referred to him as 'common', he becomes dissatisfied with the life that he leads at the forge. Pip soon begins to feel that the life of a blacksmith is not good enough for him and he starts to be quite snobbish. When he finds out that he is to come into a great fortune, Pip is very quick to drop the people who had been his friends and family in case they embarrass him when he is a gentleman. He feels some pangs of guilt about this, but does it anyway.

Pip is eager to learn to become a gentleman. He is a good pupil but becomes a snob in the process. When Joe visits him, he does little to put him at his ease and is embarrassed by him and ashamed of him. He deceives himself as to his reasons for failing to call on Joe and Biddy on his visits to Satis House.

He learns how to spend money freely and runs up large bills. He is aware however that he has encouraged Herbert to spend money he cannot afford and it is to his credit that he secretly arranges to help him in a business career. He later feels that this is the only good thing to have come out of his expectations.

His blind obsession with Estella and his belief that they

are destined for each other continue until the latter is shattered by the arrival of his real benefactor and by Estella's marriage to Drummle.

By helping Magwitch, Pip demonstrates selflessness and compassion, and the truth about his good fortune and its origins brings him humility. He is prepared to return to the forge to make an honest living and believes he would like to settle down with Biddy. However, this plan is forestalled by Joe and Biddy's marriage and he goes abroad, convinced that he will remain a bachelor. His chance meeting with Estella after eleven years seems to offer the possibility of happiness after all.

JOE

Gentle
Honest
Faithful

A simple, honest blacksmith who has married Pip's sister. He acts as Pip's companion during the boy's early years and his clear, basic values make him stand out from the more devious characters around him. He loves Pip but never tries to stand in the boy's way, even when Joe is cast aside by the child he has helped to bring up.

Joe continues to be the decent and honest character that he was at the start. His simplicity and his language provide some of the humour in the novel but it is his kindness and his loyalty which shine through. He is always charitable in his response to Pip's neglect. He cares for Pip when he is ill but he knows that there is a gap between them which can never be fully closed since Pip has become a gentleman. He has a simple dignity and knows that he is seen at his best in his place of work.

We know he will be a good husband to Bibby and a father to little Pip. He deserves the happiness he has found and which Pip envies but does not begrudge him.

Miss Havisham

Miss Havisham is a bitter old woman. She wants to take revenge on all men for the wrong that was done to her by one man. She sits in the clothes she should have worn for her wedding and is surrounded by decaying things in a darkened room. She has adopted a young girl, Estella, whom she plans to use to exact her revenge.

Miss Havisham delights in the way that Estella torments Pip and likes to keep her relatives guessing as to whom she will leave her money when she dies.

Bitter woman

Miss Havisham continues with her plan to use Estella as an instrument of revenge on the male sex until she comes to realise she has created a monster. She accuses Estella of being hard and ungrateful but Estella says she cannot give her love as she was never given it herself. She tries to undo some of the harm she has done by helping Pip with his plan for Herbert and she leaves her cousin Matthew a legacy on Pip's recommendation. At the end of her life she is distraught with guilt for what she has done to Estella and to Pip.

Estella

In the first stage of the novel, she is a beautiful young girl. She has been brought up as a young lady, but uses her education to talk down to Pip and make him feel inferior. Estella is cruel to Pip yet loyal to Miss Havisham. She is bitter and twisted due to the strange upbringing she has received from Miss Havisham. Estella does not fully realise that she is being used by the old woman and that she is, herself, little more than an agent for Miss Havisham's revenge.

Beautiful but heartless

Estella has been educated as an accomplished and sophisticated young lady. She warns Pip time and again that she has no heart and can never love anyone. She

tells Pip that he is the only one to be so warned and that she makes fools of all the other men. She seems to become tired of this way of life and is almost self-destructive in her determination to marry such a brutal and ill-mannered man as Bentley Drummle. Even Miss Havisham tries to dissuade her. At the end of the novel, she is a widow and has little property left. Her hard experiences seem to have softened her, and she implies that she regrets having rejected Pip's love for her.

She is contrite and humble as she confesses that she realises what she threw away when she rejected Pip's love. She feels that the best she can hope for is that they can be friends. She is too humble to expect more.

ABEL MAGWITCH

Led hard life Proud to have made Pip a gentleman

At first, like Pip, we are repelled by Magwitch's coarse appearance and rough habits but as we learn of his awful brutal life we become more sympathetic towards him. His pride in the gentleman he has created is touching. Pip notices that his character softens and he forms a strong affection for the convict. Magwitch feels that Pip is a replacement for the child he lost. In a very moving scene, Pip tells the dying convict that his daughter is alive and is a beautiful lady.

Through Magwitch we are shown that the legal system in the early nineteenth century worked against the poor and uneducated. Compeyson was able to wriggle free while Magwitch suffered the full penalties for his crimes. Pip's loyalty towards Magwitch redeems Pip in our eyes.

JAGGERS

Cautious
Cunning
'Steel trap'

Jaggers, a London lawyer, first appears in the novel when he meets Pip on the stairs of Satis House. He then visits the boy some years later to tell him that he is to come into a fortune. Jaggers knows all along who Pip's mysterious benefactor really is, but never gives the secret away.

Jaggers is king in the world of criminal law. Even the magistrates are frightened of him. Wemmick, his clerk compares him to a steel trap. He is very careful never to commit himself and will not allow people to tell him things he does not want to hear. After the truth is disclosed about Magwitch and after Pip challenges him about the identity of Estella's parents, he does reveal a more human side to his character. He had given Estella for adoption because he felt moved to save at least one child from the fate of so many he had seen pass through the legal system. He also hints that he too may have had 'poor dreams' when Pip refers to his own love for Estella.

HERBERT

Herbert is a perfect gentleman. He is tactful and kind when teaching Pip table manners. He is a true and honest friend to Pip, and a delightful companion, sympathising with his troubles, supporting him in his attempt to flee with Magwitch and saving his life at the limekiln on the marshes. He truly deserves to be happily married to Clara and successful in his career.

WEMMICK

Wemmick provides some of the humour in the novel, the dry lawyer's clerk who leads a double life as the whimsical architect and smallholder of Walworth. Even his employer, Jaggers, knows nothing of this Walworth life. Much of Wemmick's private life is devoted to looking after and entertaining 'the Aged', his old deaf father. In London he is well-known as Jaggers's man and acts as an intermediary between Jaggers and his criminal clients. He shows great kindness towards Pip but likes to confine any personal business to Walworth. His great motto is: always look after portable property.

OTHER CHARACTERS

Bentley Drummle

A fellow student at Matthew Pocket's. He shows himself to be surly, bad-tempered and unsociable. He is arrogant and a bully. Drummle is a rival for Estella's affections and he finally persuades her to marry him. After treating Estella very badly he dies in a riding accident involving a horse he has beaten.

Orlick

Joe's assistant at the forge, Orlick is bitterly resentful of Pip once the boy becomes the apprentice. He has a hot temper and it is only Joe's superior strength that keeps him in check.

His sinister presence makes itself felt throughout the story. He also resents Pip as he thinks the boy has thwarted his attempts to woo Biddy and has caused him to lose his job at Miss Havisham's. Orlick is in league with Compeyson for some time and has helped him in his plot against Magwitch. He finally imprisons and nearly murders Pip, after having confessed to the attack on Pip's sister. He escapes when Pip is rescued. The last we hear of him is that he is in jail for robbing Pumblechook.

Biddy

Biddy is an intelligent girl with moderate ambitions; she wants to be the local schoolteacher. She sees that Pip's ambition will bring him a good deal of heartache. She becomes Joe's housekeeper and eventually marries him. She resents the way that Pip neglects Joe and frequently acts as his conscience. In the early stage of the novel she might well be in love with Pip. Biddy is a good-hearted girl and she appreciates Joe's kindness and simple integrity.

Pumblechook A moderately successful corn-chandler who visits the forge to see Mrs Joe in particular. He has the annoying habit of firing mathematical problems at Pip. Pumblechook is generally insufferable, pompous and opinionated. He delivers the message that Pip is to play at Miss Havisham's and thereafter becomes a local legend as the man who made Pip's fortune.

Wopsle He begins as the church clerk, but even then he is not satisfied with remaining on the sidelines. He is forever boasting that he would deliver better sermons than the vicar. Thwarted in his ambition to become a clergyman he takes to the stage in London where he enjoys mixed success in some rather odd performances. His greatest claim to fame is his version of *Hamlet* which is greeted with barracking and interruption by the audience. He means well but has little sense of his own ridiculous behaviour.

Mrs Joe Pip's older sister, she is married to Joe Gargery and has brought Pip up 'by hand'. She feels hard done by and both Pip and Joe are victims of her violent temper. She defers only to her relative Pumblechook, the corn-chandler. After she is attacked by Orlick she becomes a helpless object of pity.

There are two major points to note about Charles Dickens's use of language in *Great Expectations*;

1 Character names: the names of Charles Dickens's characters give an idea of their character. This is known as characternym (see Literary Terms). Consider the type of person represented by the following:

- Pumblechook – full of his own importance and rather foolish
- Jaggers – a strong willed man who is not to be crossed
- Wopsle – spends his time trying to be important, but his attempts fail in a humorous way

Other novels have characters such as:

- Mr Bumble (*Oliver Twist*) – an officious, 'bumbling' man who abuses the power of his position
- Mr Gradgrind (*Hard Times*) – a stern man who believes that people can be treated like machines

2 Perhaps the most striking use of language in this novel comes in the form of speech. Charles Dickens is a master of characterisation and much of this is done through the way the characters themselves speak. Here are some examples of the way speech is used in the novel:

Joe Gargery is made to seem endearing through his humorous manner of speech:

'I'm oncommon fond of reading, too ...
Oncommon. Give me a good book, or a good newspaper, and sit me down afore a good fire, and I ask no better.'

This conversation is about reading, but Joe can read little more than single letters:

'Here, at last, is a J-O, Joe, how interesting reading is!'

This technique of depicting speech phonetically (as it would be said – see Literary Terms) is also used to give a comic edge to Magwitch's words:

'You young dog, what fat cheeks you ha' got. Darn me if I couldn't eat 'em, and if I han't half a mind to 't!'

and

'I've done wonderful well. There's others went out alonger me as has done well too, but no man has done nigh as well as me. I'm famous for it.'

When representing Wopsle's performance of *Hamlet* in Chapter 31, Charles Dickens uses a mock heroic tone. He deliberately writes about unimportant events as though they were extremely important. This is done to bring humour to the situation.

Charles Dickens uses descriptive language to convey the mood of a particular scene. After Pip's meeting with the convict in Chapter 1, the landscape and the weather take on a sinister aspect that the boy had not noticed before:

'The marshes were just a long black horizontal line then, … and the sky was just a row of long angry red lines and dense black lines intermixed.'

All of these techniques combine to give a quality of richness to the writing in *Great Expectations*.

PART FOUR

STUDY SKILLS

HOW TO USE QUOTATIONS

One of the secrets of success in writing essays is the way you use quotations. There are five basic principles:

- Put inverted commas at the beginning and end of the quotation
- Write the quotation exactly as it appears in the orginal
- Do not use a quotation that repeats what you have just written
- Use the quotation so that it fits into your sentence
- Keep the quotation as short as possible

Quotations should be used to develop the line of thought in your essays. Your comment should not duplicate what is in your quotation. For example:

Pip tells us how he came to be called Pip when he says, 'I called myself Pip, and came to be called Pip'.

Far more effective is to write:

Pip tells us that because he could not pronounce his full name 'I called myself Pip, and came to be called Pip'.

The most sophisticated way of using the writer's words is to embed them into your sentence:

The fact that Estella says that Pip has 'coarse hands' and wears 'thick boots' upsets him and shows us how insensitive Estella can be.

When you use quotations in this way, you are demonstrating the ability to use text as evidence to support your ideas – not simply including words from the original to prove you have read it.

Everyone writes differently. Work through the suggestions given here and adapt the advice to suit your own style and interests. This will improve your essay-writing skills and allow your personal voice to emerge.

The following points indicate in ascending order the skills of essay writing:
- Picking out one or two facts about the story and adding the odd detail
- Writing about the text by retelling the story
- Retelling the story and adding a quotation here and there
- Organising an answer which explains what is happening in the text and giving quotations to support what you write

....

- Writing in such a way as to show that you have thought about the intentions of the writer of the text and that you understand the techniques used
- Writing at some length, giving your viewpoint on the text and commenting by picking out details to support your views
- Looking at the text as a work of art, demonstrating clear critical judgement and explaining to the reader of your essay how the enjoyment of the text is assisted by literary devices, linguistic effects and psychological insights; showing how the text relates to the time when it was written

The dotted line above represents the division between lower and higher level grades. Higher-level performance begins when you start to consider your response as a reader of the text. The highest level is reached when you offer an enthusiastic personal response and show how this piece of literature is a product of its time.

Coursework essay

Set aside an hour or so at the start of your work to plan what you have to do.

- List all the points you feel are needed to cover the task. Collect page references of information and quotations that will support what you have to say. A helpful tool is the highlighter pen: this saves painstaking copying and enables you to target precisely what you want to use.
- Focus on what you consider to be the main points of the essay. Try to sum up your argument in a single sentence, which could be the closing sentence of your essay. Depending on the essay title, it could be a statement about a character: Mr Jaggers is very careful to be exact in what he says, 'There is a certain tutor, of whom I have some knowledge, … I don't recommend him, observe; because I never recommend anybody'; an opinion about setting: I think that the churchyard surrounded by the lonely marshes creates an eerie atmosphere, especially as it is getting dark; or a judgement on a theme: The inhumane treatment of prisoners is an important theme in the novel. Pip treats a convict kindly and is rewarded for it, whereas the penal system treats the same convict very harshly.

- Make a short essay plan. Use the first paragraph to introduce the argument you wish to make. In the following paragraphs develop this argument with details, examples and other possible points of view. Sum up your argument in the last paragraph. Check you have answered the question.
- Write the essay, remembering all the time the central point you are making.
- On completion, go back over what you have written to eliminate careless errors and improve expression. Read it aloud to yourself, or, if you are feeling more confident, to relative or friend.

If you can, try to type your essay, using a word processor. This will allow you to correct and improve your writing without spoiling its appearance.

Examination essay

The essay written in an examination often carries more marks than the coursework essay even though it is written under considerable time pressure.

In the revision period build up notes on various aspects of the text you are using. Fortunately, in acquiring this set of York Notes on *Great Expectations*, you have made a prudent beginning! York Notes are set out to give you vital information and help you to construct your personal overview of the text.

Make notes with appropriate quotations about the key issues of the set text. Go into the examination knowing your text and having a clear set of opinions about it.

In most English Literature examinations, you can take in copies of your set books. This is an enormous advantage although it may lull you into a false sense of security. Beware! There is simply not enough time in an examination to read the book from scratch.

In the examination

- Read the question paper carefully and remind yourself what you have to do.
- Look at the questions on your set texts to select the one that most interests you and mentally work out the points you wish to stress.
- Remind yourself of the time available and how you are going to use it.
- Briefly map out a short plan in note form that will keep your writing on track and illustrate the key argument you want to make.
- Then set about writing it.
- When you have finished, check through to eliminate errors.

To summarise,
these are the
keys to success:

- **Know the text**
- **Have a clear understanding of and opinions on the storyline, characters, setting, themes and writer's concerns**
- **Select the right material**
- **Plan and write a clear response, continually bearing the question in mind**

Sample essay plan

A typical essay question on *Great Expectations* is followed by a sample essay plan in note form. This does not present the only answer to the question, merely one answer. Do not be afraid to include your own ideas and leave out some of those in the sample! Remember that quotations are essential to prove and illustrate the points you make.

What are the results of Miss Havisham's desire for revenge?

Part 1   We first see her in the semi-derelict Satis House. She has deliberately let the house fall into bad repair because of the disappointment of her wedding day.

Part 2   She feeds her revenge by never allowing herself to forget what had happened to her, for example:

- Wearing the wedding dress
- Allowing the wedding feast to rot around her
- Stopping the clocks at the moment of her abandonment
- Keeping daylight out of the house

She torments her greedy, grasping relatives, the Pockets. She uses Pip in this as she lets them believe that Pip is to be her heir and that they will get nothing.

Part 3 — Miss Havisham adopts Estella and brings her up with the sole intention of exacting revenge on the male sex. No real thought is given to the way this will affect Estella. Initially she brings Pip to the house for Estella to practise on. This only hurts his feelings at first, but begins to change his life as he falls in love with Estella. It makes him ashamed of Joe and the forge.

Part 4 — Miss Havisham knows very well that Pip thinks for a very long time that she is his benefactress. She also lets him believe that she intends him for Estella. This is cruel as Miss Havisham knows that Estella has been brought up to despise men and that consequently, she could never make Pip happy.

Part 5 — She begins to realise that she has created an awful person when she complains that Estella shows her no affection. When Pip declares his love for Estella she finally feels remorse for what she has done. To make amends she tries to delay Estella's wedding to Drummle.

Part 6 — She helps Pip in his scheme to further Herbert's business career. On Pip's recommendation she leaves some money to Matthew Pocket, the only relative who had told her the truth about her wedding.

Part 7 — Having wasted more than half of her own life she finally regrets having partially destroyed the lives of Estella and Pip.

Make a plan as shown above and attempt these questions.

1 Examine the development of Pip's character brought about by the changes in his fortunes.

2 Does Pip deserve such kind-hearted friends as Joe Gargery, Biddy and Herbert Pocket? Explain fully the reasons for your answer.

3 How do our views of Magwitch change in the course of the novel and what do you learn from this about Charles Dickens's attitude towards the penal system?

4 Many characters in the novel show that money is no replacement for personal relationships. Discuss this idea with reference to any two of the following:
- Miss Havisham
- Bentley Drummle
- Estella
- Magwitch
- Pip

PART FIVE

CULTURAL CONNECTIONS

BROADER PERSPECTIVES

You may find some of the following works helpful when you are studying *Great Expectations*.

Film

David Lean's film of *Great Expectations* (1946) is probably the best of the film versions of the story available. This film is particularly good for studying atmosphere and characterisation.

David Lean's film of *Oliver Twist* (1948) – another Charles Dickens novel – gives a good insight into the life of the criminal underclass in London.

Written works

A Trampwoman's Tragedy (1902) is a poem by Thomas Hardy. The subject matter of the poem is very similar to the story of Molly. The poem can be found in *Chosen Poems of Thomas Hardy*, edited by James Gibson (Macmillan, 1978).

Look Back in Anger (Penguin Plays, 1956) is a play by John Osborne in which a young man struggles to come to terms with his role in society and with the problems of social class.

Room at the Top (Penguin Classics, 1957) is a novel by John Braine in which the hero is an unscrupulous young man who marries for wealth and social position.

David Copperfield (Penguin Classics, 1996 – first published 1850) is a novel by Charles Dickens. It deals with many of the same issues as *Great Expectations* does. The hero learns important lessons by way of a series of relationships and experiences.

It might also be worth looking at any references to publications such as *The Police Gazette* or *The Newgate Calendar*. There were many such cheap, true-life crime magazines printed in Victorian England. These were extremely popular and reflect an obsession with gory murders and cruel punishments.

alliteration a sequence of repeated consonantal sounds which are close together. The matching consonants are usually at the beginning of words. Alliteration may be used to stress a point or to bring humour to what is being said.

characternym a name given to a character which carries suggestions about that person's manner or appearance.

diction the writer's choice of words. You should consider why particular words have been chosen for a certain occasions and what effect the words have, either separately or together. When Pip asks Estella in Chapter 33 whether Mr Jaggers had any charge of her, she replies 'God forbid!'. This is very different to simply saying 'no'. The phrase 'God forbid' communicates clearly that Estella would hate the prospect of Mr Jaggers being responsible for her.

imagery an image is a picture in words. There are two obvious kinds of imagery – simile and metaphor. Imagery is used extensively by writers, indeed it is difficult to say very much without using imagery.

metaphor a description of one thing in terms of something else. When Mr Trabb presents a roll of cloth to Pip, Charles Dickens writes that he was 'tiding it out' on the counter. This is a metaphor; the cloth is flowing along the counter like the tide flows.

pathos the depiction of events which evoke in the reader strong feelings of pity or sorrow e.g. the death of Magwitch.

phonetically writing words as they are spoken, not in conventional spelling. Dickens uses this method to illustrate dialect – often with humorous effects.

simile a direct comparison of one thing to another. When Pip is to be sent to Miss Havisham's for the first time he says, 'I was put into clean linen like a young penitent into sackcloth'. A simile will always contain 'like', 'as' or some other linking word.

style how a writer says something. The poet Robert Frost said, 'All the fun's in how you say a thing'. The style that a writer adopts depends very much on his own personality and on what his intentions are. Charles Dickens has Pip adopt a mock-heroic style when reporting on Wopsle's *Hamlet*. This shows that Pip thinks the performance is poor and unintentionally funny.

TEST ANSWERS

TEST YOURSELF (Part One)

A
··· 1 The convict (Chapter 1)
2 Pumblechook (Chapter 4)
3 Joe (Chapter 7)
4 Estella (Chapter 8)
5 Biddy (Chapter 17)
6 Mr Jaggers (Chapter 18)
7 Pip (Chapter 18)

TEST YOURSELF (Part Two)

A
··· 1 Herbert Pocket (Chapter 21)
2 Pip (Chapter 22)
3 Wemmick (Chapter 25)
4 Estella (Chapter 33)

5 Magwitch (Chapter 39)
6 Molly (Chapter 25)
7 Bentley Drummle (Chapter 26)

TEST YOURSELF (Part Three)

A
··· 1 Bentley Drummle (Chapter 43)
2 Miss Havisham (Chapter 44)
3 Pip (Chapter 44)
4 Miss Havisham (Chapter 49)
5 Wemmick (Chapter 51)
6 Orlick (Chapter 53)
7 Herbert Pocket (Chapter 55)
8 Magwitch (Chapter 56)

NOTES

GCSE and equivalent levels (£3.50 each)

Harold Brighouse
Hobson's Choice

Charles Dickens
Great Expectations

Charles Dickens
Hard Times

George Eliot
Silas Marner

William Golding
Lord of the Flies

Thomas Hardy
The Mayor of Casterbridge

Susan Hill
I'm the King of the Castle

Barry Hines
A Kestrel for a Knave

Harper Lee
To Kill a Mockingbird

Arthur Miller
A View from the Bridge

Arthur Miller
The Crucible

George Orwell
Animal Farm

J.B. Priestley
An Inspector Calls

J.D. Salinger
The Catcher in the Rye

William Shakespeare
Macbeth

William Shakespeare
The Merchant of Venice

William Shakespeare
Romeo and Juliet

William Shakespeare
Twelfth Night

George Bernard Shaw
Pygmalion

John Steinbeck
Of Mice and Men

Mildred D. Taylor
Roll of Thunder, Hear My Cry

James Watson
Talking in Whispers

A Choice of Poets

Nineteenth Century Short Stories

Poetry of the First World War

FORTHCOMING TITLES IN THE SERIES

Advanced level (£3.99 each)

Margaret Atwood
The Handmaid's Tale

Jane Austen
Emma

Jane Austen
Pride and Prejudice

William Blake
Poems/Songs of Innocence and Songs of Experience

Emily Brontë
Wuthering Heights

Geoffrey Chaucer
Wife of Bath's Prologue and Tale

Joseph Conrad
Heart of Darkness

Charles Dickens
Great Expectations

F. Scott Fitzgerald
The Great Gatsby

Thomas Hardy
Tess of the D'Urbervilles

Seamus Heaney
Selected Poems

James Joyce
Dubliners

William Shakespeare
Antony and Cleopatra

William Shakespeare
Hamlet

William Shakespeare
King Lear

William Shakespeare
Macbeth

William Shakespeare
Othello

Mary Shelley
Frankenstein

Alice Walker
The Color Purple

John Webster
The Duchess of Malfi

Future Titles in the York Notes Series

Chinua Achebe
Things Fall Apart

Edward Albee
Who's Afraid of Virginia Woolf?

Jane Austen
Mansfield Park

Jane Austen
Northanger Abbey

Jane Austen
Persuasion

Jane Austen
Sense and Sensibility

Samuel Beckett
Waiting for Godot

John Betjeman
Selected Poems

Robert Bolt
A Man for All Seasons

Charlotte Brontë
Jane Eyre

Robert Burns
Selected Poems

Lord Byron
Selected Poems

Geoffrey Chaucer
The Franklin's Tale

Geoffrey Chaucer
The Knight's Tale

Geoffrey Chaucer
The Merchant's Tale

Geoffrey Chaucer
The Miller's Tale

Geoffrey Chaucer
The Nun's Priest's Tale

Geoffrey Chaucer
The Pardoner's Tale

Geoffrey Chaucer
Prologue to the Canterbury Tales

Samuel Taylor Coleridge
Selected Poems

Daniel Defoe
Moll Flanders

Daniel Defoe
Robinson Crusoe

Shelagh Delaney
A Taste of Honey

Charles Dickens
Bleak House

Charles Dickens
David Copperfield

Charles Dickens
Oliver Twist

Emily Dickinson
Selected Poems

John Donne
Selected Poems

Douglas Dunn
Selected Poems

George Eliot
Middlemarch

George Eliot
The Mill on the Floss

T.S. Eliot
The Waste Land

T.S. Eliot
Selected Poems

Henry Fielding
Joseph Andrews

E.M. Forster
Howards End

E.M. Forster
A Passage to India

John Fowles
The French Lieutenant's Woman

Elizabeth Gaskell
North and South

Oliver Goldsmith
She Stoops to Conquer

Graham Greene
Brighton Rock

Graham Greene
The Heart of the Matter

Graham Greene
The Power and the Glory

Thomas Hardy
Far from the Madding Crowd

Thomas Hardy
Jude the Obscure

Thomas Hardy
The Return of the Native

Thomas Hardy
Selected Poems

L.P. Hartley
The Go-Between

Nathaniel Hawthorne
The Scarlet Letter

Ernest Hemingway
A Farewell to Arms

Ernest Hemingway
The Old Man and the Sea

Homer
The Iliad

Homer
The Odyssey

Gerard Manley Hopkins
Selected Poems

Ted Hughes
Selected Poems

Aldous Huxley
Brave New World

Henry James
Portrait of a Lady

Ben Jonson
The Alchemist

Ben Jonson
Volpone

James Joyce
A Portrait of the Artist as a Young Man

John Keats
Selected Poems

Philip Larkin
Selected Poems

D.H. Lawrence
The Rainbow

D.H. Lawrence
Selected Stories

D.H. Lawrence
Sons and Lovers

D.H. Lawrence
Women in Love

Laurie Lee
Cider with Rosie

Christopher Marlowe
Doctor Faustus

Arthur Miller
Death of a Salesman

John Milton
Paradise Lost Bks I & II

John Milton
Paradise Lost IV & IX

Sean O'Casey
Juno and the Paycock

George Orwell
Nineteen Eighty-four

John Osborne
Look Back in Anger

Wilfred Owen
Selected Poems

Harold Pinter
The Caretaker

Sylvia Plath
Selected Works

Alexander Pope
Selected Poems

Jean Rhys
Wide Sargasso Sea

William Shakespeare
As You Like It

William Shakespeare
Coriolanus

William Shakespeare
Henry IV Pt 1

William Shakespeare
Henry IV Pt II

William Shakespeare
Henry V

William Shakespeare
Julius Caesar

William Shakespeare
Measure for Measure

William Shakespeare
Much Ado About Nothing

William Shakespeare
A Midsummer Night's Dream

William Shakespeare
Richard II

William Shakespeare
Richard III

William Shakespeare
Sonnets

William Shakespeare
The Taming of the Shrew

William Shakespeare
The Tempest

William Shakespeare
The Winter's Tale

George Bernard Shaw
Arms and the Man

George Bernard Shaw
Saint Joan

Richard Brinsley Sheridan
The Rivals

R.C. Sherriff
Journey's End

Muriel Spark
The Prime of Miss Jean Brodie

John Steinbeck
The Grapes of Wrath

John Steinbeck
The Pearl

Tom Stoppard
Rosencrantz and Guildenstern are Dead

Jonathan Swift
Gulliver's Travels

John Millington Synge
The Playboy of the Western World

W.M. Thackeray
Vanity Fair

Mark Twain
Huckleberry Finn

Virgil
The Aeneid

Derek Walcott
Selected Poems

Oscar Wilde
The Importance of Being Earnest

Tennessee Williams
Cat on a Hot Tin Roof

Tennessee Williams
The Glass Menagerie

Tennessee Williams
A Streetcar Named Desire

Virginia Woolf
Mrs Dalloway

Virginia Woolf
To the Lighthouse

William Wordsworth
Selected Poems

W.B. Yeats
Selected Poems

York Notes – the Ultimate Literature Guides

York Notes are recognised as the best literature study guides.
If you have enjoyed using this book and have found it useful, you
can now order others directly from us – simply follow the ordering
instructions below.

HOW TO ORDER

Decide which title(s) you require and then order in one of the following
ways:

Booksellers
All titles available from good bookstores.

By post
List the title(s) you require in the space provided overleaf,
select your method of payment, complete your name and
address details and return your completed order form and
payment to:

Addison Wesley Longman Ltd
PO BOX 88
Harlow
Essex CM19 5SR

By phone
Call our Customer Information Centre on 01279 623923 to
place your order, quoting mail number: HEYN1.

By fax
Complete the order form overleaf, ensuring you fill in your
name and address details and method of payment, and fax it
to us on 01279 414130.

By e-mail
E-mail your order to us on awlhe.orders@awl.co.uk listing
title(s) and quantity required and providing full name and
address details as requested overleaf. Please
quote mail number: HEYN1. Please do not
send credit card details by e-mail.

York Notes Order Form

Titles required:

Quantity	Title/ISBN	Price

Sub total _____

Please add £2.50 postage & packing _____

(*P & P is free for orders over £50*) _____

Total _____

Mail no: HEYN1

Your Name _____

Your Address _____

_____

Postcode _____ Telephone _____

Method of payment

☐ I enclose a cheque or a P/O for £_____ made payable to
Addison Wesley Longman Ltd

☐ Please charge my Visa/Access/AMEX/Diners Club card
Number _____ Expiry Date _____
Signature _____ Date _____

(please ensure that the address given above is the same as for your credit card)

Prices and other details are correct at time of going to press but may change without notice. All orders are subject to status.

☐ *Please tick this box if you would like a complete listing of Longman Study Guides (suitable for GCSE and A-level students)*

York Press

Longman

Addison
Wesley
Longman